ESSE...

Paris: Regions and Best places to see

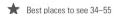

⭐ Best places to see 34–55

🔲 Featured sight

Original text by Elisabeth Morris
Updated by Penny Phenix

© Automobile Association Developments Limited 2007
First published 2007

ISBN-10: 0-7495-4966-1
ISBN-13: 978-0-7495-4966-4

Published by AA Publishing, a trading name of Automobile Association Developments Limited, whose registered office is Fanum House, Basing View, Basingstoke, Hampshire RG21 4EA.
Registered number 1878835.

A CIP catalogue record for this book is available from the British Library

Colour separation: MRM Graphics Ltd
Printed and bound in Italy by Printer Trento S.r.l.

A02694
Maps in this title produced from map data © Tele Atlas N.V. 2005
Transport map © Communicarta Ltd, UK

About this book

Symbols are used to denote the following categories:

➕ map reference to maps on cover

✉ address or location

☎ telephone number

🕐 opening times

✋ admission charge

🍴 restaurant or café on premises
   or nearby

🚇 nearest underground train station

🚌 nearest bus/tram route

🚉 nearest overground train station

✈ nearest airport

ℹ tourist information

❓ other practical information

↔ other places of interest nearby

➤ indicates the page where you will
   find a fuller description

This book is divided into six sections.

The essence of Paris pages 6–19
Introduction; Features; Food and Drink;
Short Break including the 10 Essentials

Planning pages 20–33
Before You Go; Getting There; Getting
Around; Being There

Best places to see pages 34–55
The unmissable highlights of any visit
to Paris

Best things to do pages 56–81
Great cafés; stunning views; places to
take the children and more

Exploring pages 82–165
The best places to visit in Paris,
organized by area

Excursions pages 166–183
Places to visit out of town

Maps

All map references are to the maps on
the covers. For example, Notre-Dame
has the reference ➕ 21K – indicating
the grid square in which it can be found.

Prices

An indication of the cost of restaurants
and cafés at attractions is given by €
signs: €€€ denotes higher prices, €€
denotes average prices, € denotes lower
prices.

Hotel prices

Price are per room per night: € budget
(under €100); €€ moderate (€100–€200);
€€€ expensive to luxury (over €200)

Restaurant prices

Price for a three-course meal per person
without drinks: € budget (under €30); €€
moderate (€30–€75); €€€ expensive
(over €75)

Contents

The essence of...

Paris is order, harmony, beauty and elegance – the result of bold town planning that was particularly successful in marrying tradition and innovation, sometimes with stunning effects, as in the case of the stark glass pyramid erected in front of the Louvre.

Paris is also passion, youthful energy and a stimulating cultural life.

But Paris is above all the capital of good living: the best of French cuisine, an enticing choice of gastronomic specialities from various countries, the glamorous world of haute couture and eccentric fashion, and a sparkling nightlife.

features

Paris may seem straightforward and orderly to the first-time visitor as it unfolds its wealth of stately monuments, but it is in fact a complex city and its beauty has many facets. Besides the vast open vistas there are picturesque villages like Saint-Germain-des-Prés, Le Marais or Montmartre where you may suddenly come across a tiny square steeped in a romantic old-world atmosphere or be confronted with a bold modern sculpture defiantly competing with a medieval masterpiece. However, it is the overall sense of harmony that pervades these contrasting features and confers on the city a unique homogeneity.

Paris is a compact, densely populated city and the pace of life is notoriously hectic. Fortunately, the city has its quiet spots, full of charm and mystery, ideal for relaxing after a head-spinning shopping spree in boulevard Haussmann or a marathon visit to the Louvre.

GEOGRAPHY

● Situated at the heart of northern France, some 250km (155 miles) from the sea, Paris lies on the banks of the meandering River Seine.

THE CITY
● The city is small and compact, entirely surrounded by the *boulevard périphérique*, a congested 35km-long (22-mile) dual carriageway. Green spaces cover an area of 366ha (904 acres) excluding Bois de Boulogne and Bois de Vincennes and there is one tree for every four Parisians.

GREATER PARIS
● The surrounding area, known as the *banlieue*, includes densely populated suburbs, dormitory towns and traditional villages scattered through the green belt, as well as several new towns. The whole region enjoys a reasonably dry climate, fairly cold in winter, hot and sunny in summer.

ADMINISTRATION
● Paris is a municipality administered by a council and a mayor like any other town in France, but it is also a *département* (county) headed by a *préfet*.
● Paris is divided into 20 *arrondissements* numbered from 1 to 20 starting from the Louvre in the historic centre.

POPULATION
● The city has just over 2 million inhabitants but nearly 11 million people, almost one-fifth of the French population, live in Greater Paris.

THE OLDEST...
● The oldest bridge is the pont Neuf (New Bridge!) dating from 1578.
● The oldest church is St-Germain-des-Prés, built in the 11th century.
● The oldest houses date from the 15th century; the Musée de Cluny is one of them (➤ 90).
● The oldest tree, planted in 1601, is in the square Viviani, on the Left Bank opposite Notre-Dame.

THE ESSENCE OF PARIS

food & drink

In France, eating is an art that reaches its highest expression in Paris, for here the diversity and know-how of traditional regional cuisine are combined with a creative spirit stimulated by a strong cosmopolitan influence. In recent years, a growing awareness of the need for healthier living has prompted the invention of nouvelle cuisine and contributed to change the Parisians' eating habits.

EATING PARISIAN STYLE

The traditional French breakfast of bread, butter and jam with a large cup of *café au lait* (white coffee) has to a large extent given way to cereals and milk with black coffee, tea or chocolate. The traditional fresh croissants are often a weekend treat, when people breakfast *en famille*.

The majority of working people have lunch out. Cafés and bistros overflow onto the pavements in spring and summer and overworked waiters are continually calling out *steak frîtes* (steak and chips) at the tops of their voices, as Parisians order their favourite lunchtime dish. Some of the trendiest places to have lunch are *bars à huîtres* (oyster bars, serving a variety of seafood) and cyber cafés where you can have a snack and a drink while surfing the Internet.

Dinner at home around 8pm is the first relaxing meal of the day, enjoyed with family or friends; it starts with hors-d'oeuvre, finishes with cheese or a sweet and may include a freshly prepared dish bought from a local *traiteur* (delicatessen), accompanied by a glass of wine.

SHOPPING FOR FOOD

Parisians are still very fond of their local street markets where they can buy fresh vegetables and fruit as well as cheese, *charcuterie* (deli), fish and meat. One traditional item which is still going strong is the *baguette*, the light and crisp bread that is better in Paris than anywhere else in France!

EATING OUT

Eating out is one of the Parisians' favourite forms of entertainment, as conviviality is as important as the food itself. Friday night and Saturday night are the most popular evenings, while families with children tend to go out for Sunday lunch. Parisian cuisine includes a wide choice of regional and traditional dishes, although the tendency nowadays is to lighten sauces. Typical Parisian dishes are *soupe à l'oignon gratinée* (onion soup *au gratin*) and *pieds de cochon* (grilled pig's trotters), traditionally eaten near Les Halles when this was the chief food market in Paris. Oysters and seafood in general are also very popular, judging by the numerous take-away seafood stalls outside restaurants in the city centre.

Wine is a must with any good meal, preceded by an aperitif, which may consist of port, whisky or champagne. A *digestif* (brandy, Cointreau or any other liqueur) is served with coffee at the end of the meal.

MUSÉE DU VIN

Anyone interested in wine should visit this museum, appropriately housed in the old cellars of Passy Abbey. It illustrates the history of wine in France and the main wine-producing areas, and has a collection of tools, bottles and wax figures. An added inducement is the opportunity for some wine tasting.

✉ Rue des Eaux, 5 square Charles Dickens, 75016 ☎ 01 45 25 63 26 🕐 Tue–Sun 10–6 👆 Moderate; free for visitors eating in the restaurant 🍴 Bistro (€) 🚇 Passy ❓ Guided tours, bookshop, gift shop 🚌 72

short break

If you have only a short time to visit Paris and would like to take home some unforgettable memories you can do something local and capture the real flavour of the city. The following suggestions will give you a wide range of sights and experiences that won't take very long, won't cost very much and will make your visit very special. If you only have time to choose just one of these, you will have found the true heart of the city.

● **Take a boat trip along the Seine** from the pont de l'Alma and admire the stately monuments whose splendour is dramatically enhanced at night by powerful spotlights. It's a great way to view some of the city's major sights from a different and magical perspective, and you can see many famous landmarks in just over an hour.

● **Climb to the top of the Tour Eiffel** for an aerial view of Paris; it's a guaranteed thrill from the panoramic lift (elevator). Visit early in the morning or late at night to avoid the queues, but for the best views come an hour before sunset. You can even get your postcards stamped with the famous Eiffel Tower postmark at the post office on level one.

● **Take a morning walk through the attractive Jardin du Luxembourg** and stand beside the romantic Fontaine de Médicis, named after Marie de Médicis, wife of Henri IV, who commissioned the Palais du Luxembourg.

● **Sit outside Les Deux Magots café** in boulevard St-Germain, on the Left Bank, and watch the world go by (► 59). This Paris institution, named after the wooden statues of two Chinese dignitaries (*magots*) inside the café, has managed to retain its literary feel. Street bustle peaks around lunchtime and from 6pm.

- **Stand on the pont de la Tournelle** near Notre Dame: look downriver for panoramic views of 'old Paris' (Île de la Cité and beyond) and upriver for contrasting views of 'new Paris' (Bercy and the Institut du Monde Arabe; ➤ 88).

- **Stroll along the *quais*** and browse through the *bouquinistes'* stock of old prints and books (➤ 50–51). These rickety old green booths are very much a part of the Parisian riverscape.

- **Take the funicular to Sacré-Coeur** at the top of Montmartre for stunning views of the city (➤ 158–159). It runs all day and costs one métro ticket each way.

- **Go to the colourful Moulin-Rouge** show and discover the glamour of traditional Parisian entertainment (➤ 157). The 'Red Windmill' has been immortalized in the posters and paintings of the artist Toulouse-Lautrec.

- **Stand on the place de la Concorde** at night and look up the Champs-Elysées (➤ 38–39). The illuminated avenue, gently rising towards the Arc de Triomphe, offers one of the most perfect urban vistas in the world. The 3,200-year-old obelisk at its centre is the city's most ancient monument.

- **Mingle with Parisians** doing their daily shopping in the street markets along the rue Mouffetard (Quartier Latin), or on Sundays, buying organic food on boulevard Raspail. Nothing beats it for local colour.

Planning

Before You Go

WHEN TO GO

JAN	FEB	MAR	APR	MAY	JUN	JUL	AUG	SEP	OCT	NOV	DEC
7°C	7°C	10°C	16°C	17°C	23°C	25°C	26°C	21°C	16°C	12°C	8°C
45°F	45°F	50°F	61°F	63°F	73°F	77°F	79°F	70°F	61°F	54°F	46°F

🔵 High season   ⚪ Low season

Temperatures are the average daily maximum for each month. The best time to visit Paris is June, a glorious month when the days are longest, with the most sunshine and average daytime temperatures a comfortable 23°C (73°F). The city reaches peak tourist capacity in July. August sees the Parisian exodus to the countryside leaving the city emptier than usual. It is the hottest, most humid month and the city is prone to sudden storms. September and October have a high percentage of crisp days and clear skies, but rooms can be difficult to find as this is the peak trade-fair period. Winter temperatures rarely drop below freezing, but it rains frequently, sometimes with hail, from November to January.

WHAT YOU NEED

● Required
○ Suggested
▲ Not required

Some countries require a passport to remain valid for a minimum period (usually at least six months) beyond the date of entry – check before you travel.

	UK	Germany	USA	Canada	Australia	Ireland	Netherlands	Spain
Passport (or National Identity Card where applicable)	●	●	●	●	●	●	●	●
Visa (regulations can change – check before you travel)	▲	▲	▲	▲	▲	▲	▲	▲
Onward or Return Ticket	▲	▲	▲	▲	▲	▲	▲	▲
Health Inoculations (tetanus and polio)	▲	▲	▲	▲	▲	▲	▲	▲
Health Documentation (► 23, Health)	●	●	●	●	●	●	●	●
Travel Insurance	○	○	○	○	○	○	○	○
Driving Licence (national)	●	●	●	●	●	●	●	●
Car Insurance Certificate	○	○	n/a	n/a	n/a	○	○	○
Car Registration Document	●	●	n/a	n/a	n/a	●	●	●

ADVANCE PLANNING
WEBSITES
● Paris Tourist Office: **www.**parisinfo.com (this site also has information for visitors with disabilities)
● Paris Tourisme: **www.**paris-tourism.com
● French Tourist Office: **www.**franceguide.com

TOURIST OFFICES AT HOME
In the UK French Government Tourist Office ✉ 178 Piccadilly, London W1J 9AL ☎ 09068 244123

In the USA French Tourist Office ✉ 444 Madison Avenue, 16th Floor, New York, NY10022 ☎ 514/288-1904 French Government Tourist Office ✉ 9454 Wilshire Boulevard, Suite 715, Beverly Hills, CA90212 ☎ 514/288-1904

In Australia French Tourist Office ✉ Level 13, 25 Bligh Street, Sydney, NSW 2000 ☎ (02) 9231 5244

In Canada French Tourist Office ✉ 1981 avenue McGill, College Suite 490, Montréal H3A 2W9 ☎ 514/288-2026

HEALTH ADVICE
Insurance Nationals of EU countries can obtain medical treatment at reduced cost in France with the relevant documentation (EHIC – European Health Insurance Card), although private medical insurance is still advised and is essential for all other visitors.

Dental services As for general medical treatment (see Insurance, opposite), nationals of EU countries can obtain dental treatment at reduced cost. Around 70 per cent of standard dentists' fees are refunded. However, private medical insurance is advised for all visitors.

TIME DIFFERENCES

GMT 12 noon	France 1pm	Spain 1pm	USA (NY) 7am	USA (West Coast) 4am	Sydney 10pm

France is on Central European Time, one hour ahead of Greenwich Mean Time (GMT +1). From late March, when clocks are put forward one hour, until late October, French summer time (GMT +2) operates.

WHAT'S ON WHEN

The events listed here are liable to change from one year to the next and in the case of major festivals, there is often more than one venue. Dates also vary slightly.

PARIS

June *Festival Chopin:* An annual tribute to the Romantic composer at the Orangerie de Bagatelle in the heart of the Bois de Boulogne.
Fête de la Musique: On 21 June, Paris's squares, gardens and streets come alive with hundreds of musicians.
Festival de Théâtre: Open-air theatre in English and French in the Jardin de Pré Catelan in the Bois de Boulogne.

June–July *Paris Jazz Festival:* Open-air concerts in the Parc Floral de Paris, Bois de Vincennes.
14 July: Military parade down the Champs-Elysées, fireworks and popular ball to celebrate National Day.

July–August *Fête des Tuileries:* Jardin des Tuileries becomes a fairground (begins end of June). *Paris, Quartier d'Eté:* Open-air music, plays and dance.

September *Biennale Internationale des Antiquaires:* Biennial international antiques display (even years); last two weeks September. *La Villette Jazz Festival:* Jazz in the Grande Halle and Parc de la Villette.

October *Foire Internationale d'Art Contemporain:* Exhibition of contemporary art. *Mondial de l'Automobile:* International motor-car show every two years (even years).

December *Salon Nautique International:* International boat show.

NATIONAL HOLIDAYS

JAN	FEB	MAR	APR	MAY	JUN	JUL	AUG	SEP	OCT	NOV	DEC
1		(1)	(1)	3(4)	(1)	1	1			2	1

1 Jan	New Year's Day
Mar/Apr	Easter Sunday and Monday
1 May	May Day
May	VE (Victory in Europe) Day
6th Thu after Easter	Ascension Day
May/Jun	Whit Sunday and Monday
14 Jul	Bastille Day
15 Aug	Assumption Day
1 Nov	All Saints' Day
11 Nov	Remembrance Day
25 Dec	Christmas Day

Banks, businesses, museums and most shops (except *boulangeries*) are closed on these days.

ÎLE-DE-FRANCE

April–May *Salon des Antiquaires de Rambouillet:* Antiques fair.

May–June *Festival de Saint-Denis:* Symphonic concerts take place in Saint-Denis basilica.
Fête Médiévale: Medieval pageant, siege warfare demonstrations, tournaments in Provins.
Le Mois Moière: Theatre, music and street entertainment in parts of the city of Versailles.

June–July *Festival d'Auvers-sur-Oise:* Singing, piano and chamber music.

July–August *Fête des Loges de Saint-Germain-en-Laye:* A fair held in Saint-Germain forest.

July–September *Festival de l'Orangerie de Sceaux:* Chamber music festival in parc de Sceaux.

August *Fête de la Saint-Louis à Fontainebleau:* An ancient royal tradition celebrated by fireworks at the château.

September *Fête du Cheval Fontainebleau:* International gathering of horse lovers.
Barbizon au temps des peintres: Recalls 1848–70, when the Forêt de Fontainebleau drew artists to Barbizon.

September–mid-October *Festival d'Île-de-France:* Concerts and shows in castles, abbeys and churches throughout the region.

Getting There

Ticket prices tend to be highest in spring and summer (Easter to September). City break packages may offer even more savings if a Saturday night is included. Check with the airlines, travel agents and Internet for best deals and offers.

BY AIR

Paris has two main airports – Roissy Charles de Gaulle (☎ 01 48 62 22 80) where most international flights arrive, and Orly (☎ 01 45 31 16 20). Numerous carriers operate direct flights from Canada and the US, including American Airlines, Delta and Air Canada. From the UK, British Airways, British Midland and easyJet operate regular services; from Australia, Qantas and Continental are the major carriers. France's national airline, Air France (☎ 0820 820 820 in France; 0870 142 4343 in the UK; 800/237-2747 in the US; **www.**airfrance.com) has scheduled flights from Britain, mainland Europe and beyond, to both main airports. Approximate flying times to Paris: London (1 hour), Dublin (1.5 hours), New York (8 hours), West Coast USA (12 hours), Vancouver (10 hours), Montréal (7.5 hours), Sydney (23 hours), Auckland (21 hours).

It's 23km (14 miles) from Roissy Charles de Gaulle Airport to the city centre and takes between 35 minutes and 1 hour, depending on public transport used. It's 14km (8.5 miles) from Orly Airport to the city centre and takes between 25 and 45 minutes depending on public transport used.

BY RAIL

The Eurostar passenger train service (tel: 08705 186186 in Britain; **www.**eurostar.com) from London Waterloo via the Channel Tunnel to Paris Gare du Nord takes 3 hours. This is probably the easiest way to come to Paris as the train brings you into the heart of the city. There are six major railway stations, each handling traffic to different parts of France and

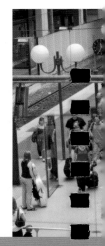

Europe – Gare de Lyon, Gare du Nord, Gare de l'Est, Gare St-Lazare, Gare d'Austerlitz and Gare Montparnasse. French Railways operates high-speed trains (TGV – *Train à Grande Vitesse*) to Paris from main stations throughout France.

BY SEA

Ferry companies operate regular services from England and Ireland to France, with rail links to Paris. Crossing time: 35 minutes to 6 hours (England); 14–18 hours (Ireland).

DRIVING

Driving is on the right.

Speed limits on toll motorways

(autoroutes) **130kph/80mph** (**110kph/68mph** when wet). Non-toll motorways and dual carriageways: **110kph/68mph** (**100kph/62mph** when wet). Paris ring road *(périphérique)*: **80kph/50mph**. Speed limits on country roads: **90kph/56mph** (**80kph/50mph** when wet). Speed limits on urban roads: **50kph/31mph**.

Seatbelts must be worn in front seats at all times and in rear seats where fitted.

Random breath-testing takes place. Never drive under the influence of alcohol.

Leaded petrol is sold as *essence super* (98 octane). Unleaded is available in two grades: *essence sans plomb* (95 octane) and *essence super sans plomb* (98 octane). Diesel *(Gasoil or Gazole)* is also readily available. In Paris filling stations can be hard to spot, often consisting of little more than a few kerb-side pumps.

If you break down on a motorway *(autoroute)* use the orange-coloured emergency phones (located every 2km/1.2 miles) to contact the breakdown service.

Getting Around

PUBLIC TRANSPORT

INTERNAL FLIGHTS
Air France is the leading domestic airline – information (☎ 08 20 82 08 20). Daily departures from Orly and Roissy/Charles-de-Gaulle airports connect Paris with major French cities/towns in an average flight time of one hour.

RER
The RER (pronounced 'ehr-oo-ehr') is the fast suburban rail service, which also serves the city centre. There are five lines *(lignes):* A, B, C, D and E and the RER is connected with the métro and SNCF suburban network. Services run 5.30am to midnight, with trains every 12 minutes.

MÉTRO
Paris's underground with over 300 stations ensures you are never more than 500m (550yds) from a métro stop. Lines are numbered 1 to 14 and are known by the names of the stations at each end. Follow the orange *correspondance* signs to change lines. The métro runs daily 5.30am to 12.30am.

BUSES
Buses are a good way of seeing Paris (especially route 24), although traffic can be very heavy. Bus stops show the numbers of buses that stop there. Buses run 6.30am to 8.30pm with a reduced service on Sunday and after 8.30pm. Bus tickets are the same as those for the métro.

BOAT
The Batobus river shuttle (☎ 01 44 11 33 99) that plies the Seine provides an unusual view of Paris. It stops at the Eiffel Tower, Musée d'Orsay, St-Germain-des-Prés, Notre-Dame, Jardin des Plantes, Hôtel de Ville, the Louvre and the Champs-Elysées; Feb–Dec 10–10 (to 7pm in winter).

TAXIS
Taxis can be hailed if you see one with its roof light on. Taxis are metered with a surcharge for

luggage, journeys after 10pm and before 6.30am, and for going from and to stations and airports. Queues can be very long, particularly at railway stations.

CAR

If your car breaks down in Paris, contact the 24-hour repair service (☎ 01 45 31 16 20).

CAR RENTAL

Car-rental companies have desks at Roissy/Charles-de-Gaulle and Orly airports, and in Paris itself. Car rental is expensive, but airlines and tour operators offer fly-drive, and French Railways (SNCF) have train/car, packages that are cheaper than renting locally.

ARRONDISSEMENTS

Paris is divided into 20 districts or *arrondissements*, which spiral clockwise from the city centre. The central *arrondissements* are numbered from 1 to 8:

1 (75001): heart of the Right Bank, centred on the Louvre and the Île de la Cité.
2 (75002): the commercial district around the Opéra.
3 and **4** (75003 and 75004): the Marais district and the Île St-Louis.
5 (75005): the Latin Quarter and the Left Bank.
6 (75006): the St-Germain district.

7 (75007): residential Faubourg St-Germain and the Tour Eiffel.
8 (75008): the chic district of broad avenues radiating out from the Arc de Triomphe.

CONCESSIONS

Students/youths Holders of an International Student Identity Card (ISIC) are entitled to half-price admission to museums and sights and discounted air and ferry tickets, plus inexpensive meals in some student cafeterias. Those under 26, but not a student, with the International Youth Travel Card (or GO 25 Card) qualify for similar discounts as ISIC holders.

Senior citizens Visitors aged over 60 can get discounts (up to 50 per cent) in museums, on public transport and in places of entertainment. Discounts apply to holders of the Carte Senior, which can be purchased from the Abonnement (ticket) office of any main railway station. Without the card, show your passport and you may still get the discount.

Being There

TOURIST OFFICES

HEAD OFFICE

● Office de Tourisme de Paris (Paris Tourism Bureau), 25 rue des Pyramides, 75001 Paris, ☎ 08 92 68 30 00 (omit the initial 0 when calling from outside France) **www**.paris-touristoffice.com

BRANCHES IN PARIS

● Opéra-Grands Magasins Mon–Sat 9am–6.30pm
● Gare de Lyon 🕐 Mon–Sat 8am–6pm
● Gare du Nord 🕐 Daily 8am–6pm
● Montmartre (21 place du Tertre) 🕐 Daily 10am–7pm

● Tour Eiffel (Eiffel Tower) 🕐 Late Mar–Oct: daily 11am–6.40pm

PARIS ÎLE-DE-FRANCE

● Carrousel du Louvre (lower level), ☎ 01 44 50 19 98/08 26 16 66 66 **www**.pidf.com 🕐 Daily 10am–7pm
● Disneyland Resort Paris, place des Passagers-du-Vent, Marne-la-Vallée, 77705, ☎ 01 60 43 33 33 🚈 RER line A, Marne-la-Vallée–Parc Disneyland

EMBASSIES AND CONSULATES

UK ☎ 01 44 51 31 00
Germany ☎ 01 53 83 45 00
USA ☎ 01 43 12 22 22
Netherlands ☎ 01 40 62 33 00
Spain ☎ 01 44 43 18 00

TELEPHONES

All telephone numbers in France comprise 10 digits. Paris and Île de France numbers all begin with 01. There are no area codes, simply dial the number. Most public phones use a phone-card *(télécarte)* sold in units of 50 or 120 from France Telecom shops, post offices, tobacconists and railway stations. Cafés have phones that take coins. Cheap rates generally apply Mon–Fri 7pm–8am, Sat–Sun all day.

OPENING HOURS

- Shops
- Offices
- Banks
- Museums/Monuments
- Churches
- Pharmacies

In addition to the times shown above, some shops close between noon and 2pm and all day Sunday and Monday. Large department stores open from 9.30am to 6.30pm and until 9 or 10pm one or two days a week. Food shops open 7am to 1.30pm and 4.30 to 8pm; some open Sunday until noon.

Some banks have extended hours, including Saturday morning but most close weekends. Museum and monument opening times vary, but national museums close Tuesday (except the Trianon Palace, the Musée d'Orsay and Versailles which close Monday), while other museums usually close Monday.

EMERGENCY TELEPHONE NUMBERS

Police 17
Fire 18
Ambulance 15
Doctor (24-hour call out) 01 47 07 77 77

INTERNATIONAL DIALLING CODES

Dial 00 followed by:
UK: 44
Ireland: 353
USA/Canada: 1
Australia: 61

Germany: 49
Spain: 34

POSTAL SERVICES

Post offices are identified by a yellow or brown 'La Poste' or 'PTT' sign. The main office at 52 rue du Louvre is open 24 hours. The branch at 71 avenue des Champs-Elysées is open Mon–Fri 9am–7.30pm, Sat 10am–7pm.

ELECTRICITY

The power supply in Paris is 220 volts. Sockets accept two-round-pin (or increasingly three-round-pin) plugs, so an adaptor is needed for most non-Continental appliances. A transformer is needed for appliances operating on 110–120 volts.

CURRENCY AND EXCHANGE

Currency The French unit of currency is the euro (€). Coins are issued in denominations of 1, 2, 5, 10, 20 and 50 cents and €1 and €2. There are 100 cents in €1. Notes (bills) are issued in denominations of €5, €10, €20, €50, €100, €200 and €500.

Exchange You can exchange travellers' cheques at some banks and at bureaux de change at airports, main railway stations or in some department stores, and exchange booths. All transactions are subject to a hefty commission charge, so you may prefer to rely on cash and credit cards. Travellers'

cheques issued by American Express and Visa can also be changed at many post offices.

Credit cards are widely accepted in shops, restaurants and hotels. Visa, MasterCard and Diners Club cards with four-digit PINs can be used in most ATMs.

HEALTH AND SAFETY

Sun advice July and August (when most Parisians leave the city) are the sunniest (and hottest) months. If 'doing the sights' cover up or apply a sunscreen and take plenty of fluids.

Drugs Pharmacies – recognized by their green cross sign – have highly qualified staff who are able to offer medical advice, provide first aid and prescribe a wide range of drugs, though some are available by prescription *(ordonnance)* only.

TIPS/GRATUITIES

Yes ✓ No ✗		
Hotels (service included)	✓	change
Restaurants (service included)	✓	change
Cafés/bars (service included)	✓	change
Taxis	✓	€1
Tour guides	✓	€1
Porters	✓	€1
Hairdressers	✓	€1
Cloakroom attendants	✓	15–30c
Theatre/cinema usherettes	✓	30c
Toilets	✓	change

Safe water It is quite safe to drink tap water in Paris and all over France, but never drink from a tap marked *eau non potable* (not drinking water). Mineral water is fairly cheap and widely available.

Petty crime, particularly theft of wallets and handbags is fairly common in Paris. Be aware of innocent, scruffy-looking children – they may be working the streets in gangs, fleecing tourists. Report loss or theft to the Police Municipale (blue uniforms). To be safe:
● Watch your bag on the métro, in areas like the Champs-Elysées and Beaubourg and in museum queues.
● Cars should be well-secured.
● Put valuables in your hotel safe.

PHOTOGRAPHY
What to photograph: Paris's monumental buildings and animated Parisians drinking in pavement cafés.
Where you need permission to photograph: certain museums will allow you to photograph inside. In churches with mural paintings and icons where flashlight is required, ask permission first.
Where to buy film: shops and photo laboratories sell the most popular brands and types of film. Rapid film development is possible but quite expensive.

CLOTHING SIZES

France	UK	Rest of Europe	USA	
46	36	46	36	
48	38	48	38	
50	40	50	40	
52	42	52	42	
54	44	54	44	Suits
56	46	56	46	
41	7	41	8	
42	7.5	42	8.5	
43	8.5	43	9.5	
44	9.5	44	10.5	
45	10.5	45	11.5	Shoes
46	11	46	12	
37	14.5	37	14.5	
38	15	38	15	
39/40	15.5	39/40	15.5	
41	16	41	16	
42	16.5	42	16.5	Shirts
43	17	43	17	
36	8	34	6	
38	10	36	8	
40	12	38	10	
42	14	40	12	
44	16	42	14	Dresses
46	18	44	16	
38	4.5	38	6	
38	5	38	6.5	
39	5.5	39	7	
39	6	39	7.5	
40	6.5	40	8	Shoes
41	7	41	8.5	

Best places to see

Restaurants Bars

1

Centre Georges Pompidou

www.centrepompidou.fr

This spacious and convivial art centre, in the heart of historic Paris, houses under one roof all forms of modern and contemporary art.

With 25,000 visitors a day, the Centre Georges Pompidou is now one of Paris's top sights. Yet at the time it was built, close to the historic Marais which is famous for its elegant architecture, the 'refinery', as Rogers and Piano's post-modern building was nicknamed, deeply shocked French people. In fact, the revolutionary concept of this open-plan 'house of culture for all' ensured its success and brought life back to the district. The centre has had its first major face-lift and been completely refurbished inside; its main asset, the Musée National d'Art Moderne, reached by the external escalator, gained extra exhibition space in the process. The museum is dedicated to the main trends of art from 1905 to the present day. Modern art is displayed on level 5. Particularly well represented are Fauvism (Dufy, Derain, Matisse), Cubism (Braque, Picasso, Léger), Dadaism, Surrealism (Dali, Miró), Expressionism (Soutine, Kirchner, Modigliani and to a lesser extent Chagall), various forms of abstract art (Kandinsky, Klee, but also Poliakoff, Dubuffet and the CoBrA movement), and pre-1960 American painting. The collections of contemporary art (level 4) include exponents of the new realism (Arman, César), of Pop Art (Warhol), of Minimalist art (Sol Lewitt, Buren) and of monochromes (Manzoni, Klein).

The centre also houses a library, the Institute for Acoustic and Musical Research, the Centre for Industrial Creation, a large exhibition hall, a children's workshop and a reconstruction of Brancusi's workshop.

✚ 12A ✉ Place Georges-Pompidou, 75004 ☎ 01 44 78 12 33 🕐 Centre: Wed–Mon. Modern art museum and exhibitions: 11–9. Library: weekdays 12–10; weekends 11–10. Brancusi workshop 2–6 🖐 Free access; museum: moderate (includes Brancusi workshop, children's workshop and level 6) 🍴 Restaurant (€€), café and snack bar 🚇 Rambuteau, Hôtel de Ville 🚌 38, 47, 75 ❓ Audioguides, ATM, shops

2 Les Champs-Elysées

www.monum.fr

AVENUE
des
CHAMPS ELYSEES
8ème

For most visitors this prestigious avenue epitomizes French elegance, but it is also a dazzling place of entertainment and a luxury shopping mall.

In the late 17th century, André Le Nôtre designed a gently rising alleyway as an extension of the Jardin des Tuileries. This later lost its rustic appearance and became a fashionable avenue lined with elegant restaurants and cafés. Nowadays it is the traditional venue for a variety of events such as the Paris Marathon, the arrival of the Tour de France and the march past on 14 July, which celebrates France's national day. But 'les Champs' (the fields) is also a place where people of all ages just relax and feel alive.

The lower section, stretching from the place de la Concorde (with breathtaking views along the whole length of the avenue) to the Rond-Point des Champs-Elysées, is laid out as an English-style park shaded by imposing chestnut trees. On the left are the Grand and Petit Palais, two temples of the arts, while on the right is a monument to the French Resistance hero, Jean Moulin, who was reburied in the Panthéon on 19 December 1964.

The upper section stretches from the Rond-Point, designed by Le Nôtre, to the Arc de Triomphe. This is the 'modern'

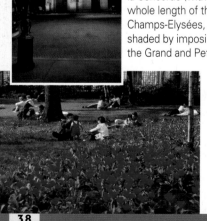

part of the avenue, with its pavements now revamped and restored to their former comfortable width. Banks, cinemas, airline offices, car showrooms and large cafés spread out on the pavements, lining the way to the place de l'Etoile. Fashion boutiques cluster along the arcades running between the Champs-Elysées and the parallel rue de Ponthieu. Some shops remain open well into the night and the bustle only quietens down in the early hours of the morning.

✚ 5C ✉ Avenue des Champs Elysées, 75008 🍴 Choice of restaurants (€–€€€) Ⓜ Concorde, Champs-Elysées-Clemenceau, Franklin-D Roosevelt, George V, Charles-de-Gaulle-Etoile 🚌 32, 42, 73

3 La Grande Arche de la Défense

www.grandearche.com

Symbolically guarding the western approach to the city, the Grande Arche is both a recognition of tradition and a bold step towards the future.

From the arch's roof top (110m/360ft above ground), accessible by the exterior lift, a marvellous view unfolds in a straight line along an axis to the Arc de Triomphe and, beyond, to the Obelisk at place de la Concorde and to the Louvre, extending the magnificent vista opened up by Le Nôtre. The arch was inaugurated in 1989 for the bicentenary celebrations of the French Revolution and is now a major tourist attraction. The stark simplicity of its architectural outline and the materials used are definitely contemporary, while its sheer size is a marvel of modern technology. The Danish architect, Otto von Spreckelsen, built a perfect hollow concrete cube covered over with glass and white

Carrara marble. Steps lead up to the central platform, where the lifts are to be found.

The arch dominates a vast square, known as Le Parvis, decorated with colourful sculptures, including a red 'stabile' by Calde, and flanked by another remarkable building: the CNIT (Centre of New Industries and Technology), shaped like an upside-down-shell, which serves mainly as a conference centre but is also a pleasant meeting place for business people. There are several cafés and a branch of the FNAC, the French equivalent of Virgin stores, stocking a large selection of CDs covering a wide spectrum of musical tastes.

Opposite, there is a huge shopping centre known as Les Quatre Temps, which has some of the best shopping bargains in Paris. Its focal point is the vast hypermarket Auchan.

✚ 1E (off map) ✉ 1 parvis de la Défense, 92044 Paris-La Défense ☎ 01 49 07 27 57 (Grande Arche) 🚇 Grande Arche: daily 10–7 🛗 Lift (elevator) of Grande Arche: moderate 🍴 Rooftop restaurant, snackbars and cafés in Les Quatre Temps shopping centre (€) and in the CNIT (€ and €€) 🚇 La Défense 🚌 73, Balabus in summer ❓ Video presentation, guided tours, shops

4 Les Invalides

www.invalides.org

This is one of Paris's most imposing architectural ensembles, built around two churches and housing several museums.

The Hôtel National des Invalides was commissioned by Louis XIV as a home for wounded soldiers. It is a splendid example of 17th-century architecture, the classical austerity of its 200m-long (656ft) façade being offset by the baroque features of the Église du Dôme, with its gilt dome glittering above the slate roofs of the stone buildings. The huge esplanade filling the gap between the river and the monumental entrance enhances the majesty of the building.

The museums are accessible from the arcaded main courtyard. The Musée de l'Armée is one of the richest museums of its kind in the world. It contains weapons from all over the world, armour and uniforms, mementoes of famous generals, paintings, documents and models. Particularly striking is the comprehensive permanent exhibition devoted to World War II.

The Musée des Plans-Reliefs is a fascinating collection of models of fortified French towns, originally started at Louis XIV's request.

On the far side of the courtyard is the entrance to St-Louis-des-Invalides, the soldiers' church, which contains a colourful collection of flags brought back from various campaigns.

The magnificent Église du Dôme, built by Jules Hardouin-Mansart, is a striking contrast: an elegant façade with two tiers of Doric and Corinthian columns and an imposing gilt dome surmounted by a slender lantern. The splendid interior decoration is enhanced by the marble floor. The open circular crypt houses Napoleon's red porphyry tomb.

✚ 14L ✉ Esplanade des Invalides, 75007 ☎ 01 44 42 37 72 🕐 6 Apr to mid-Jun and late Sep daily 10–5; mid-Jun to mid-Sep daily 10–7. Closed 1 Jan, 1 May, 1 Nov, 25 Dec 👋 Moderate 🍽 Restaurant (€) Ⓜ Invalides, La Tour Maubourg, Varenne 🚌 28, 63, 69, 80, 82, 84, 87, 92, 93 ❓ Audiovisual shows, guided tours, shops

5 Le Louvre

www.louvre.fr

This former royal palace, which celebrated its bicentenary in 1993, is today one of the largest museums in the world.

THE PALACE

Excavations carried out in 1977 under the Cour Carrée, the courtyard surrounded by the oldest part of the palace, led to the discovery of the original castle built around 1200 by King Philippe-Auguste. The tour of the foundations of this medieval Louvre, including the base of the keep, the moat and the outer wall, starts from the main entrance hall under the glass pyramid.

The first palace, built by Pierre Lescot in the style of the Italian Renaissance, was enlarged round the Cour Carrée and along the Seine during the following 200 years. Louis XIV enclosed the Cour Carrée with the stately colonnade that faces the Church of St-Germain-l'Auxerrois. Soon afterwards, however, the King left for Versailles and the palace was neglected by the royal family and the court.

Building was resumed by Napoleon, who built part of the north wing and erected the exquisite Arc de Triomphe du Carrousel. During the second half of the 19th century, Napoleon III completed the Louvre along its rue de Rivoli side.

THE MUSEUM

The collections are divided into eight departments:
● Egyptian Antiquities include a pink granite *Sphinx from Tanis*, a huge *head of Amenophis IV-Akhenaten* and the famous *Seated Scribe*.

● The most remarkable exhibits in the Oriental Antiquities Department must be the *Assyrian winged bulls*.

● The Greek, Etruscan and Roman Antiquities department contains many masterpieces: don't miss the *Vénus de Milo*, *Winged Victory* and Graeco-Roman sculpture in the Salle des Cariatides.

● The painting collections comprise a fine selection from the Italian school (Fra Angelico, Leonardo da Vinci, Giotto, Veronese, Titian, Raphael), the French school (Poussin, Watteau, Georges de la Tour), the Dutch school (Rembrandt, Rubens, Vermeer) and Spanish masters (Murillo, Goya and El Greco).

● French sculpture is well represented and includes works by Goujon, Houdon and Pradier.

● Objets d'art, displayed to full advantage in the Richelieu wing, include beautiful tapestries and historic items such as Charlemagne's sword.

● The department of Graphic Art houses drawings, prints and watercolours.

● The newly created department of Islamic Art will gradually expand over the next few years.

✚ 10A ✉ 99 rue de Rivoli, 75001. Main entrance via pyramid ☎ Recorded info: 01 40 20 51 51; reception desk: 01 40 20 53 17; visitors with disabilities: 01 40 20 59 90 🕐 Thu–Sun 9–6, Mon and Wed 9am–9.45pm. Closed 1 Jan, 1 May, 11 Nov, 25 Dec ✋ Moderate until 3pm, reduced fee after 3 and Sun, free on 1st Sun of month. To avoid a long wait, buy your ticket in advance online 🍴 Restaurants (€ and €€) and cafés below pyramid and in Carrousel du Louvre 🚇 Palais-Royal/Musée du Louvre 🚌 21, 24, 27. 39, 48, 68, 69, 72, 81, 95 ❓ Guided tours, lectures, concerts, film shows, shops

6 Notre-Dame

www.cathedraldeparis.com

This masterpiece of Gothic architecture is one of Paris's most famous landmarks and one of France's most visited religious monuments.

In 1163, the Bishop of Paris, Maurice de Sully, launched the building of the cathedral, which took nearly 200 years to complete. One of the architects involved was Pierre de Montreuil, who also built the nearby Sainte-Chapelle (➤ 93). Later alterations deprived the church of its rood screen and of some of its original stained glass; its statues were mutilated during the Revolution because the Commune thought they were likenesses of the kings of France; the cathedral also lost all its original bells, except the *'gros bourdon'*, known as Emmanuel, which is traditionally heard on occasions of national importance. Restoration work was carried out in the 19th century by the famous architect Viollet-le-Duc and the area round the cathedral was cleared.

From across the vast square in front of the cathedral you can admire the harmonious proportions and almost perfect symmetry of the façade. The richly decorated portals are surmounted by statues of the kings of Judaea, restored by Viollet-le-Duc. Above the central rose window, a colonnade links the elegant twin towers; there is a splendid view from the south tower, if you can face up to the 387-step climb.

The nave is 130m (426ft) long, 48m (157ft) wide and 35m (115ft) high; the side chapels are richly decorated with paintings, sculptures and funeral monuments. Note the beautiful rose window at each end of the transept. The former vestry, on the right of the chancel, houses the Cathedral Treasure, which includes a piece of the Holy Cross.

✝ 21K ✉ Place du Parvis de Notre-Dame, 75004 ☎ 01 42 34 56 10 🕐 Cathedral: daily 8–6.45; closed some religious feast days. Treasure: Mon–Sat 9.30–11.30, 1–5.30. Towers: Apr–Sep daily 9.30–7.30 (Jul–Aug Sat–Sun 9.30am–11pm); Oct–end Mar daily 10.30–5.30 🖐 Cathedral: free; treasure and towers: inexpensive 🍴 Left Bank (€–€€) 🚇 Cité, Saint-Michel 🚌 21, 24, 27, 38, 47, 85, 96

Orsay, Musée d'

www.musee-orsay.fr

Once a mainline railway station, the Musée d'Orsay has been successfully converted into one of Paris's three major art museums.

Built in 1900, the Gare d'Orsay was narrowly saved from demolition by a daring plan to turn it into a museum dedicated to all forms of art from 1848 to 1914, and intended as the chronological link between the Louvre and the Musée National d'Art Moderne. The Musée d'Orsay was inaugurated by President Mitterrand in 1986.

The main hall, with the station clock, was retained to create a sense of unity between painting, sculpture, architecture, design, photography and the cinema. The collections are spread over three levels:

● The Lower Level deals with the years from 1848 to 1880; small flights of steps lead off the central alleyway to various exhibition areas where major sculptures are displayed, including a group of graceful figures by Carpeaux entitled *La Danse*. On either side is a comprehensive collection of paintings of the same period – works by Ingres, Delacroix, Corot, Courbet and the Realists, as well as the beginning of Impressionism with early works by Monet, Manet, Pissarro and others.

● On the Upper Level is the prestigious Impressionist and post-Impressionist collection, undoubtedly the main attraction of the museum: masterpieces are by Manet *(Olympia)*, Degas *(Blue Dancers)*, Sisley *(Snow in Louveciennes)*, Renoir *(Bathers)*, Monet *(The Houses of Parliament, Rouen Cathedral)*, Cézanne *(The Card Players)*, Van Gogh *(The Church at Auvers-sur-Oise)*, Gauguin and the school of Pont-Aven, Matisse, Toulouse-Lautrec and many others.

● The Middle Level is dedicated to the period from 1870 to 1914 and includes important works by Rodin *(Balzac)*, paintings by the Nabis school, as well as a comprehensive section on art nouveau (Lalique, Gallé, Guimard, Mackintosh and Wright).

✚ 8A ✉ 62 rue de Lille (entrance rue de Légion d'Honneur), 75007 ☎ 01 40 49 48 14; 01 40 49 48 00 🕐 Tue–Sat 10–6, Sun 9–6; late night: Thu 9.45 (opens 9am Jul–Sep). Closed Mon, 1 Jan, 1 May, 25 Dec 💰 Moderate, free first Sun each month 🍽 Restaurant (€), café (€) Ⓜ Solférino 🚌 24, 63, 68, 69, 73, 83, 84, 94 ❓ Guided tours, shops, concerts, film shows

8 Les Quais

Walk along the banks of the Seine between the pont de la Concorde and the pont de Sully for some of Paris's finest views.

In 1992, the river banks from the pont d'Iéna, where the Tour Eiffel stands, to the pont de Sully, at the tip of the Île Saint-Louis, were added to Unesco's list of World Heritage Sites. Here the townscape has an indefinable charm inspired by the harmonious blend of colours: the pale greys and blues of the water and the sky, the soft green of the trees lining the embankment and the mellow stone colour of the historic buildings. Parisians have been strolling along the embankments for centuries, window-shopping, browsing through the *bouquinistes'* stalls or simply watching the activity on both sides of the river.

THE RIGHT BANK

Start from the pont du Carrousel and walk up-river past the imposing façade of the Louvre. From the pont Neuf, enjoy a fine view of the Conciergerie on the Île de la Cité, or admire the birds and exotic fish on the quai de la Mégisserie. Continue past the Hôtel de Ville towards the lovely pont Marie leading to the peaceful Île Saint-Louis. Cross over to the Left Bank.

THE LEFT BANK

The familiar green boxes of the *bouquinistes* are here as well! Admire the stunning views of Notre-Dame and its magnificent flying buttresses. The quai Saint-Michel is a favourite haunt of students looking for second-hand books. Further on, stand on the pont des Arts for a romantic view of the historic heart of Paris before walking past the stately façade of the Musée d'Orsay towards the pont de la Concorde.

✚ 20K ✉ Quai du Louvre, quai de la Mégisserie (75001), quai de Gesvres, quai de l'Hôtel de Ville, quai des Célestins (75004), quai de la Tournelle, quai de Montebello, quai St-Michel (75005), quai des Grands Augustins, quai de Conti, quai Malaquais (75006), quai Voltaire, quai Anatole-France (75007) 🍴 Restaurants and cafés along the way, particularly near place du Châtelet and place de l'Hôtel de Ville on the Right Bank, and around place St-Michel on the Left Bank (€–€€€) 🚇 Pont-Neuf, Châtelet, Hôtel de Ville, Pont-Marie, St-Michel, Solférino 🚌 24 follows the Left Bank ❓ Boat trips along the Seine from pont de l'Alma right round the islands

9 La Tour Eiffel

www.tour-eiffel.fr

Paris's most famous landmark has been towering above the city for more than a hundred years, yet its universal appeal remains constant.

The Tour Eiffel was built by the engineer Gustave Eiffel as a temporary attraction for the 1889 World Exhibition. At the time, its 300m (984ft) height made it the tallest building in the world and an unprecedented technological achievement. It met with instant success, was celebrated by poets and artists, and its spindly silhouette was soon famous all over the world. In spite of this, it was nearly pulled down when the concession expired in 1909 but was saved because of its invaluable radio aerial, joined in 1957 by television aerials. It was later raised by another 20m (66ft) to accommodate a meteorological station. The iron frame weighs 7,000 tonnes, yet the pressure it exerts on the ground is only 4kg per sq cm; 40 tonnes of paint are used to repaint it every seven years. To celebrate its one hundredth birthday, it was renovated and halogen lighting was installed making it even more spectacular at night.

There are three levels, all accessible by lift, or by stairs – first and second floors only. Information about the tower is available on the first floor (57m/187ft above ground); there are also a restaurant, a gift shop and a post office, where letters are postmarked Paris Tour Eiffel.

The second floor (115m/377ft above ground) offers fine views of Paris, several boutiques and a restaurant appropriately named Jules Verne.

For a spectacular aerial view of the capital go up to the third floor (276m/905ft above ground). There is also a reconstruction of Gustave Eiffel's study and panoramic viewing tables showing 360-degree photos of Paris with the city's landmarks.

➕ 2A ✉ Champ de Mars, 75007 ☎ 01 44 11 23 23 🕐 Jan to mid-Jun and Sep–Dec daily 9.30am–11pm, (stairs to 6); mid-Jun to Aug daily 9am–midnight ♿ Lift (elevator): 1st–2nd floors inexpensive–moderate, 3rd floor expensive 🍴 Restaurants (€–€€€) 🚇 Bir-Hakeim 🚌 42, 69, 72, 82, 87

10 ◯ La Villette

www.cite-sciences.fr
www.cite-musique.fr

The Cité des Sciences et de l'Industrie and the Cité de la Musique revitalized the outer district of La Villette, turning it into a new cultural centre.

Situated just inside the boulevard Périphérique, between the Porte de la Villette and the Porte de Pantin, the 30-ha (74-acre) parc de la Villette was laid out on the site of Paris's former abattoirs. This ultra-modern park includes two vast cultural complexes, one devoted to science and the other to music, themed gardens scattered with red metal follies and various children's activity areas. A long covered walk joins the main buildings.

CITÉ DES SCIENCES ET DE L'INDUSTRIE

The abattoirs' former auction hall was transformed into a vast scientific complex surrounded by water in which the public is both spectator and actor. 'Explora' is a permanent exhibition centred on the earth and the universe, life, languages and communication, the use of natural resources and technological and industrial developments. The Cité des Enfants is a fascinating interactive world for children aged 3 to 12. There are also a planetarium, an aquarium, a 3-D cinema, a multimedia library, a research centre, a submarine, a simulation booth (Cinaxe), in which spectators are able to live through the action of a film, and La Géode, a huge sphere equipped with a hemispherical screen that shows films on scientific subjects.

CITÉ DE LA MUSIQUE

The focal point of the Cité de la Musique is the vast square in front of the Grande Halle where concerts and exhibitions are held. On the left of the square is the new music and dance conservatory, while the triangular building on the right houses concerts halls and a museum (see Musée de la Musique ➤ 157).

🕂 28Q (off map) ✉ Cité des Sciences et de l'Industrie, parc de la Villette, 30 avenue Corentin Cariou, 75019; Cité de la Musique, 221 avenue Jean Jaurès, 75019 ☎ Cité des Sciences: 01 40 05 70 00; Cité de la Musique: information bookings 01 44 84 44 84 ⓧ Cité des Sciences: Tue–Sat 10–6, Sun 10–7; closed 1 May, 25 Dec. Cité de la Musique: Tue–Sat 12–6, Sun 10–6 ✋ Cité des Sciences: expensive; Cité de la Musique: free; museum: moderate
🍴 Restaurants nearby (€–€€) 🚇 Cité des Sciences: Porte de la Villette; Cité de la Musique: Porte de Pantin 🚌 Cité des Sciences: 75, 139, 150, 152, PC; Cité de la Musique: 75, 151, PC ❓ Cité des Sciences: exhibitions, lectures, shops; Cité de la Musique: themed tours, workshops, musical tours

Best things to do

Great cafés

Café Beaubourg
Ignore the restaurant and take a table on the terrace, which overlooks the square. It's an ideal spot for people-watching, and handy for the nearby Centre Georges Pompidou.
✉ 43 rue St-Merri, 75004 🚇 Rambuteau

Café de Flore
Cosmopolitan Café de Flore, famous as a haunt for bohemian existentialists – notably writer-philosophers Camus, Simone de Beauvoir and Sartre – is now a hugely popular tourist attraction.
✉ 172 boulevard St-Germain, 75006 🚇 St-Germain-des-Prés

Café de la Mairie
The terrace here is a super place to appreciate the French way of life, as well as to enjoy great snacks.
✉ 8 place St-Sulpice, 75006 🚇 St-Sulpice

Café Marly
Designed by Olivier Gagnère, the Café Marly has wonderful views of I M Pei's glass pyramid. The menu offers typical brasserie food with occasional modern offerings.
✉ 93 rue de Rivoli, 75001 🚇 Palais-Royal

Café Martini
This old Italian-style café, just off place des Vosges, is open till late.
✉ 11 rue du Pas de la Mule, 75004 🚇 Chemin-Vert

La Closerie des Lilas
Enjoy a drink in this intimate café where poets Baudelaire and Apollinaire and American writer Hemingway once sat. It's a pleasant place for an early evening drink on the sunny flower-filled terrace.
✉ 171 boulevard du Montparnasse, 75015 🚇 Vavin

Les Deux Magots

Les Deux Magots was made famous in the early 20th century by the likes of Picasso and the poet André Breton. It has been the popular rendezvous of almost every Paris intellectual.

✉ 6 place St-Germain-des-Prés, 75006 🚇 St-Germain-des-Prés

Fouquet's

This chic café on the Champs-Elysées is the place to spot local celebrities from French radio, TV and cinema. As with most places of this kind, it comes with a price.

✉ 99 Champs-Elysées, 75008 🚇 George V

Le Procope

An 18th-century literary café known to Voltaire and Rousseau, and now an elegant dining room. Benjamin Franklin is said to have drafted part of the American Constitution here.

✉ 13 rue de l'Ancienne-Comédie, 75006 🚇 Odéon

Le Sancerre

A traditional French café-bar, popular with the young and trendy, in Montmartre.

✉ 35 rue des Abbesses, 75018 🚇 Abbesses

Good places to have lunch

Altitude 95 (€–€€)
Brasserie with original airship décor and fabulous views over the Seine and the Trocadero.

✉ Tour Eiffel 1st floor, Champs de Mars, 75007 ☎ 01 45 55 20 04

A Priori Thé (€)
Old-world surroundings. Choose from an imaginative selection of savoury dishes, plus home-made cakes and pastries.

✉ 35–37 Galerie Vivienne, 75002 ☎ 01 42 97 48 75

Bofinger (€€)
An elegant brasserie with a charming *belle époque* setting. Serves beautifully prepared classic French dishes.

✉ 3 rue de la Bastille, 75004 ☎ 01 42 72 87 82

Brasserie de l'Île Saint-Louis (€€)
The *choucroute garnie* is excellent, as is the onion tart. Leave room for dessert.

✉ 55 quai de Bourbon, 75004 ☎ 01 43 54 02 59

Le Caveau du Palais (€€)
Atmospheric old inn with a view of lovely place Dauphine. The *confit de canard* and wood-fire grilled ribs are worth the visit.

✉ 17 place Dauphine, 75001 ☎ 01 43 26 04 28

Georges (€€–€€€)
Fabulous views of Paris from the top floor. Serves nouvelle cuisine and a delicious melt-in-the-mouth chocolate cake.

✉ Centre Georges Pompidou (6th floor), 75004 ☎ 01 44 78 47 99

Le Polidor (€)
A 19th-century bistro serving such classic French cuisine as boeuf bourguignon in the heart of the Latin Quarter.

✉ 41 rue Monsieur-le-Prince, 75006 ☎ 01 43 26 95 34

Restaurant du Palais-Royal (€€)
People come more for the peaceful setting overlooking the Jardin du Palais-Royal than for the food.
✉ 43 rue de Valois, 75001 ☎ 01 40 20 00 27

Le Toupary (€€)
Enjoy the panoramic view over the Seine from this restaurant in the famous department store.
✉ Samaritaine, 5th floor, 2 quai du Louvre, 75001 ☎ 01 40 41 29 29

La Victoire Suprême du Coeur (€€)
International vegetarian cuisine, including many vegan specialities. Good food and good service.
✉ 41 rue des Bourdonnais, 75001 ☎ 01 40 41 93 95

Excellent restaurants

Beauvilliers (€€–€€€)
Gourmet cuisine served in an elegant Napoleon III setting; terrace in summer.

✉ 52 rue Lamarck, 75018 ☎ 01 42 55 05 42 🕐 Lunch, dinner; closed Mon lunch, Sun 🚇 Lamarck Caulaincourt

Brasserie Lipp (€€)
Founded in 1880, this restaurant is always popular with the famous.

✉ 151 boulevard St-Germain, 75006 ☎ 01 45 48 53 91 🕐 Daily 🚇 St-Germain-des-Prés

La Coupole (€€)
Famous brasserie from the 1920s with its art deco setting and excellent seafood. Reasonable late-night menu (after 11pm).

✉ 102 boulevard du Montparnasse, 75014 ☎ 01 43 20 14 20 🕐 Daily 8.30am–1pm 🚇 Vavin

Le Divellec (€€€)
One of the top seafood restaurants in Paris complete with nautical décor, and very good service.

✉ 107 rue de l'Université, 75007 ☎ 01 45 51 91 96 🕐 Lunch, dinner; closed Sat, Sun and Christmas 🚇 Invalides

Grand Véfour (€€€)

Haute cuisine amid 18th-century décor with a beautiful view of the Jardin du Palais-Royal.

✉ 17 rue de Beaujolais, 75001 ☎ 01 42 96 56 27 🕓 Lunch, dinner; closed Fri night, Sat, Sun and Aug 🚇 Palais-Royal

Guy Savoy (€€€)

A true culinary experience, with delicacies such as poached-grilled pigeon and giblets in a beetroot and mushroom millefeuille.

✉ 18 rue Troyon, 75017 ☎ 01 43 80 40 61 🕓 Lunch, dinner; closed Sat lunch, Sun 🚇 Charles de Gaulle-Étoile

Jacques Cagna (€€€)

High-class traditional French cuisine in a 17th-century residence with wood panelling and beams; Dutch paintings to match.

✉ 14 rue des Grands-Augustins, 75006 ☎ 01 43 26 49 39 🕓 Lunch, dinner; closed Sat, Mon lunch, Sun 🚇 Saint-Michel

Lucas Carton (€€€)

Haute cuisine with authentic late 19th-century décor by Majorelle; good roast duck.

✉ 9 place de la Madeleine, 75008 ☎ 01 42 65 22 90 🕓 Lunch, dinner daily 🚇 Madeleine

Timgad (€€€)

Spectacular Moorish interior, innovative, exciting food and attentive service at one of France's best known Arab restaurants.

✉ 21 rue Brunel, 75017 ☎ 01 45 74 23 70 🕓 Daily 🚇 Argentine

La Tour d'Argent (€€€)

Haute cuisine in exceptional surroundings with remarkable view of Notre-Dame and the river; speciality is canard (duck) Tour d'Argent.

✉ 15–17 quai de la Tournelle, 75005 ☎ 01 43 54 23 31 🕓 Lunch, dinner; closed Mon, Tue lunch 🚇 Pont-Marie

Stunning views

Arc de Triomphe (➤ 118)

Centre Georges Pompidou (6th floor; ➤ 36–37)

Dôme of Les Invalides (➤ 43)

La Grande Arche de la Défense (➤ 40–41)

Institut du Monde Arabe (➤ 88)

Places to take the children

Cité des Sciences et de l'Industrie

This cathedral-sized science and technology museum is housed in a large former slaughterhouse in La Villette. The Cité des Enfants, for the 3–5 and 5–12 age groups, is on the ground floor. The main part of the museum, Explora, has a variety of scientific activities for all the family.

✉ 30 avenue Corentin-Cariou, 75019 ☎ Information: 01 40 05 80 00 🕐 Tue–Sat 10–6, Sun 10–7 🚇 Porte de la Villette

Jardin d'Acclimatation

Adventure park at the heart of the Bois de Boulogne.

✉ Bois de Boulogne, 75016 ☎ 01 40 67 90 82 🕐 Daily 10–6; small train from Porte Maillot on Wed, Sat, Sun, public hols 1.30–6 🚇 Sablons, Porte Maillot

Jardin des Enfants aux Halles

An adventure ground for 7- to 11-year-olds.

✉ Forum des Halles, 105 rue Rambuteau, 75001 ☎ 01 45 08 07 18 🕐 Oct–May Tue–Sun 9–12, 2–4 (Wed 10–4); Jul, Aug Tue, Thu, Fri 9–12, 2–6; Wed, Sat 10–6, Sun 1–6 🚇 Les Halles

Musée Grévin

Five hundred wax figures of the famous, from Henry VIII to Michael Jackson and Arnold Schwarzenegger!

✉ 10 boulevard Montmartre, 75009 ☎ 01 47 70 85 05 🕐 Mon–Fri 10–6.30; Sat–Sun 10–7 🚇 Rue Montmartre

Musée de la Magie

Fascinating demonstrations of magic; workshops during school holidays.

✉ 11 rue Saint-Paul, 75004 ☎ 01 42 72 13 26 🕐 Wed, Sat, Sun 2–7 🚇 Saint-Paul

Musée de la Marine
Shows for 8- to 12-year-olds, with titles such as Treasure Island, on Wednesdays.
✉ Palais de Chaillot, place du Trocadéro, 75016
☎ 01 53 06 69 53 🕐 Wed–Mon 10–6
🚇 Trocadéro

Musée National d'Histoire Naturelle
Spectacular procession of large and small animals in the Grande Galerie de l'Evolution.
✉ 57 rue Cuvier, 75005 ☎ 01 40 79 30 00
🕐 Wed–Mon 10–5 🚇 Jussieu, Gare d'Austerlitz

Parc des Buttes-Chaumont
Cave, waterfall, lake, island and suspended bridge, with playgrounds for smaller children.
✉ 5 rue Botzaris, 75019 ☎ 01 42 38 02 63
🕐 Daily 7am–9pm 🚇 Buttes-Chaumont

Parc Zoologique de Paris
Located inside the Bois de Vincennes, this is much larger than the zoo at the Jardin des Plantes.
✉ 53 avenue de Saint-Maurice, 75012 ☎ 01 44 75 20 10 (recorded information) 🕐 Daily 9–6 (6.30 Sun and public hols) 🚇 Porte Dorée

Paris-story
Audiovisual show illustrating the history of Paris through its monuments.
✉ 11 bis rue Scribe, 75009 ☎ 01 42 66 62 06
🕐 Daily 9–7 on the hour 🚇 Opéra

Activities

Walking (pedestrian areas): try the footpath along the Seine; or the quartier Montorgueil north of Les Halles.

Cycle tours: Paris à Vélo, c'est Sympa! Bicycle is one of the best ways to discover Paris. Guided tours, as well as unaccompanied bicycle and tandem rental, are available.
✉ 22 rue Alphonse Baudin, 75011 ☎ 01 48 87 60 01

Rowing: on the lake in the Bois de Boulogne, just outside the *périphérique*

Horse-back riding: Société d'Equitation de Paris Ponies and horses for children and adults.
☎ 01 45 01 20 06

Theme parks: Disneyland® Resort Paris (➤ 169), Parc Astérix (➤ 171).

Parc Floral de Paris: flower displays and medicinal plants, plus mini-golf, quad-biking and the Théatre pour Enfants (on certain days only) for the kids.
✉ Bois de Vincennes, 75012

Aquaboulevard: fun with water – toboggans and whirlpools, plus squash and tennis courts, a putting range and several restaurants and shops.
✉ 4–6 rue Louis-Armand, 75015 ☎ 01 40 60 10 00

Hot-air ballooning: experience breathtaking views of Paris's surroundings with Montgolfières Aventures.
✉ 8 Villa Hallé, 75014 ☎ 01 40 47 61 04

Roller-skating rallies: Randonnée en Rollers. A mass in-line skate through Paris held every Sunday afternoon.
☎ 01 44 54 07 44 for information

Leisure park: Base de Plein Air
Activities include sailing, riding, cycling, fishing.
✉ St-Quentin-en-Yvelines ☎ 01 30 62 20 12 🚇 RER C

a walk

along the Seine and on the Islands

This relatively compact area offers stately historic buildings, breathtaking views, provincial charm and the liveliness of a great city.

Start from the place du Châtelet on the Right Bank.

The monumental fountain was commissioned by Napoleon on his return from Egypt.

Walk along the quai de Gesvres, then across the pont Notre-Dame.

The flower market on the place Louis Lépine is a refreshing sight. On Sunday, flowers are replaced by birds.

Walk east along the embankment, turn right into rue des Ursins then left and left again.

The narrow streets of the medieval cathedral precinct have some old houses. At the tip of the island is an underground memorial to the victims of Nazi concentration camps.

Cross over to the Île Saint-Louis and turn left, following the quai de Bourbon.

Enjoy the peaceful atmosphere of this sought-after residential area.

Turn right into rue des Deux Ponts and cross over to the Left Bank. Walk west to the square Viviani then cross rue St-Jacques into rue St-Séverin.

This is one of the oldest parts of the Quartier Latin. The Gothic church of St-Séverin has a magnificent interior.

From the place St-Michel, cross back on to the Île de la Cité.

Sainte-Chapelle (➤ 93) is very close. The place Dauphine at the western end of the island is another haven of peace. Admire the view from the pont Neuf, Paris's oldest bridge.

Cross over to the Right Bank and the pont Neuf métro station.

Distance 4km (2.5 miles)
Time 2–4 hours depending on church visits
Start point Place du Châtelet 🚇 Châtelet or 🚌 21, 38, 85, 96
End point Pont Neuf 🚇 Pont Neuf or 🚌 21, 58, 67, 70
Lunch Le Vieux Bistrot ✉ 14 rue du Cloître-Notre-Dame, 75004
☎ 01 43 54 18 95

Places to be entertained

CABARET AND MUSIC HALL
Le Lido
The show put on by the famous Bluebell girls is still very effective.
It is possible to have dinner on a *bateau-mouche* followed by a
show at the Lido.

 116 bis avenue des Champs-Elysées, 75008 ☎ 01 40 76 56 10 🚇 George V

Moulin-Rouge
Undoubtedly the most famous of them all! The show still includes
impressive displays of French can-can.

✉ 82 boulevard de Clichy, 75018 ☎ 01 53 09 82 82 🚇 Blanche

CONCERT VENUES
Cité de la Musique
This new temple of classical music regularly sets new trends with
special commissions.

✉ 221 avenue Jean Jaurès, 75019 ☎ 01 44 84 45 00 🚇 Porte de Pantin

Théâtre des Champs-Elysées

Paris's most prestigious classical concert venue with top international orchestras.

✉ 15 avenue Montaigne, 75008 ☎ 01 49 52 50 00 🚇 Alma-Marceau

Théâtre du Châtelet

Classical concerts, opera performances, ballets and variety shows alternate in this 19th-century theatre that has welcomed great names such as Mahler and Diaghilev.

✉ 1 place du Châtelet, 75001 ☎ 01 40 28 28 00 🚇 Châtelet

Zénith

This huge hall is the mecca of rock concerts, a privilege it shares with the Palais Omnisports de Paris Bercy.

✉ 211 avenue Jean Jaurès, 75019 ☎ 01 42 08 60 00 🚇 Porte de Pantin

JAZZ CLUB
Caveau de la Huchette

Jazz and rock mania let loose in medieval cellars!

✉ 5 rue de la Huchette, 75005 ☎ 01 43 26 65 05 🚇 Saint-Michel

NIGHTCLUB
La Casbah

Acid jazz and house alternate on different days with dance, disco music. Exotic décor.

✉ 18–20 rue de la Forge-Royale, 75011 ☎ 01 43 71 04 39 🚇 Faidherbe-Chaligny

SPORT
Parc des Princes

The famous venue for national and international football and rugby matches.

✉ 24 rue du Commandant-Guilbaud, 75016 ☎ 01 49 48 90 00 🚇 Porte de Saint-Cloud

Museums and art galleries

Arts Asiatiques-Guimet, Musée National des

The renovated and extended Musée Guimet is now one of the most outstanding museums of Asian art in the world (▶ 118).

🕂 2C ✉ 6 place d'Iéna, 75016 ☎ 01 56 52 53 00 🚇 Boissiére, Iéna
🚌 22, 30, 32, 63, 82

Arts Décoratifs, Musée des

This fascinating museum devoted to interior design and decoration has more than 150,000 items on display (▶ 119).
www.ucad.fr

🕂 9B ✉ 107 rue de Rivoli; 75001 ☎ 01 44 55 57 50 🚇 Palais-Royal
🚌 21, 27, 39, 48, 68, 72, 81, 95

Carnavalet, Musée

The Carnavalet retraces the history of Paris from antiquity to the present day, and is worth visiting for the building alone (▶ 138).

🕂 23L ✉ 23 rue de Sévigné, 75003 ☎ 01 42 72 21 13 🚇 Saint-Paul
🚌 29, 69, 76, 96

Chaillot, Palais de

This imposing architectural complex on top of a hill overlooking the river and facing the Tour Eiffel across the pont d'Iéna offers magnificent views and houses two interesting museums (▶ 120).
www.mnhn.fr; www.musee-marine.fr

🕂 1B ✉ Place du Trocadéro, 75016 ☎ Musée de l'Homme: 01 44 05 72 72;
Musée de la Marine: 01 53 65 69 69 🚇 Trocadéro 🚌 22, 30, 32, 63, 72, 82

Grand Palais

The most strking feature is its distinctive curved glass roof, especially when it is illuminated within at night (▶ 123).

🕂 5C ✉ Galeries Nationales: avenue du Général Eisenhower, 75008; Palais de la Découverte, avenue Franklin-D-Roosevelt, 75008 ☎ Galeries Nationales: 01 44 13 17 30; Palais Découverte: 01 56 43 20 21 🚇 Champs-Elysées-Clemenceau 🚌 28, 32, 42, 72, 73, 80, 83, 93

Jeu de Paume

This airy, neoclassical building was originally commissioned by Napoleon III as an indoor court for *réal* (royal) tennis (➤ 124).

�︎ 7C ✉ 1 place de la Concorde, 75001 ☎ 01 47 03 12 52 🚇 Concorde 🚌 24, 42, 52, 72, 73, 84, 94

Marmottan-Monet, Musée

Although off the beaten track, this is a must for anyone interested in the Impressionist movement and Monet in particular (➤ 125).

�︎ 1B (off map) ✉ 2 rue Louis Boilly, 75016 ☎ 01 42 24 07 02 🚇 La Muette 🚌 22, 32, 52, 63

Moyen-Age, Musée National du

This splendid museum of medieval art, also known as the Musée de Cluny, in a 15th-century Gothic mansion, is one of the last examples of medieval domestic architecture in Paris (➤ 90).

www.musee-moyenage.fr

🚫 20K ✉ 6 place Paul Painlevé, 75005 ☎ 01 53 73 78 00; 01 53 73 78 16 🚇 Cluny-La Sorbonne 🚌 21, 27, 38, 63, 85, 86, 87

Picasso, Musée

The museum's collection consists of more than 200 paintings, sculptures, prints, drawings and ceramics (➤ 145).

www.musee-picasso.fr

🚫 23M ✉ Hôtel Salé, 5 rue de Thorigny, 75003 ☎ 01 42 71 25 21 🚇 Saint-Paul, Chemin Vert 🚌 29, 69, 75, 96

Rodin, Musée

One of the lovely mansions in the elegant Faubourg St-Germain, built by Gabriel in 1728, houses a unique collection of works by the sculptor Auguste Rodin (➤ 109).

www.musee-rodin.fr

🚫 15L ✉ 77 rue de Varenne, 75007 ☎ 01 44 18 61 10 🚇 Varenne 🚌 69, 82, 87, 92

Churches and cathedrals

Madeleine, Église de la

This immense, neoclassical church, resembling a Greek temple, with its Corinthian pillars, is one of Paris's great landmarks (➤ 124–125).

🔳 7D ✉ Place de la Madeleine, 75008 ☎ 01 44 51 69 00 🚇 Madeleine
🚌 24, 42, 52, 84, 94

La Mosquée

A gem of 20th-century European Islamic architecture, with its impressive square minaret and ornate decoration.

🔳 21H ✉ Place du Puits-de-l'Ermite, 75005 ☎ 01 45 35 97 33 🚇 Jussieu, Place Monge, Censier-Daubenton

Notre-Dame

The grandeur of this magnificent cathedral, one of the world's most beautiful examples of early Gothic architecture, never fails to inspire (➤ 46–47).

🔳 21K ✉ Place du Parvis Notre-Dame, 75004 ☎ 01 42 34 56 10 🚇 Cité, Saint-Michel

Sacré-Coeur, Basilique du

The gleaming white Basilica of the Sacred Heart, at the top of Montmartre's hill, dominates the skyline of the Butte, with views that stretch for 50km (31 miles) around the city (➤ 158–159).
www.sacre-coeur-montmartre.com

🔳 27R ✉ Place du Parvis du Sacré-Coeur, 75018 ☎ 01 53 41 89 00
🚇 Abbesses (from here walk along rue Yvonne Le Tac, then take funicular or walk up steps) 🚌 30, 54, 80, 85, Montmartrobus

Sainte-Chapelle

Sainte-Chapelle's stunning stained-glass windows, which cover an area of more than 600sq m (6,460sq ft), make it one of Paris's most beautiful churches (➤ 93).

🔳 20L ✉ 4 boulevard du Palais, 75001 ☎ 01 53 40 60 80 🚇 Cité 🚌 96

St-Etienne-du-Mont

The 15th-century Church of St-Etienne-du-Mont is an architectural mixture of Gothic Flamboyant, Renaissance and Classical styles (➤ 92).

✠ 20J ✉ Place Ste-Geneviève, 75005 ☎ 01 43 54 11 79 Ⓜ Cardinal Lemoine 🚌 84, 89

St-Eustache

Paris's second-largest church after Notre-Dame took 105 years to build. Henri de Miller's curious sculpture *L'Écoute*, stands outside (➤ 141).

✠ 11B ✉ Place du Jour, 75001 ☎ 01 42 36 31 05 Ⓜ Les Halles

St-Germain-des-Prés

The oldest church in Paris stands at the heart of the lively Left Bank district of St-Germain-des-Prés. Facing the church is the Café des Deux Magots which, like its neighbour the Café de Flore, was the favourite haunt of intellectuals, in particular Sartre and Simone de Beauvoir, immediately after World War II (➤ 109).

✠ 18L ✉ Place St-Germain-des-Prés, 75006 ☎ 01 55 42 81 33 Ⓜ St-Germain-des-Prés

St-Séverin

The Gothic Church of St-Séverin has a delightful blend of Flamboyant Gothic architecture and beautiful stained glass, which makes it worth seeking out (➤ 94).

✠ 20K ✉ 1 rue des Prêtres-St-Séverin, 75005 ☎ 01 42 34 93 50 Ⓜ Saint-Michel

St-Sulpice

The church and square of St-Sulpice form a harmonious architectural ensemble, mostly dating from the 18th century, except for part of the church and the central fountain (➤ 110).

✠ 18K ✉ Place St-Sulpice, 75006 ☎ 01 46 33 21 78 Ⓜ St-Sulpice

Places to stay

George V (€€€)

The George V offers the high levels of service you would expect from an international hotel. Many of the guest rooms have private balconies overlooking the city.

✉ 31 avenue George-V, 75008 ☎ 01 49 52 70 00; www.fourseasons.com/paris 🚇 George V

Hôtel d'Angleterre Saint-Germain-des-Prés (€€–€€€)

The largest rooms of this quiet luxury hotel overlook the secluded garden.

✉ 44 rue Jacob, 75006 ☎ 01 42 60 34 72 🚇 St-Germain-des-Prés

Hôtel Claude Bernard (€€–€€€)

A stylish 17th-century mansion in the Marais district, close to the Centre Georges Pompidou. The breakfast room has a magnificent vaulted ceiling.

✉ 43 rue des Écoles, 75005 ☎ 01 43 26 32 52 🚇 Maubert-Mutualité

Hôtel Franklin-Roosevelt (€€€)

Bright comfortable bedrooms with striking murals in the bathrooms; warm welcome.

✉ 18 rue Clément Marot, 75008 ☎ 01 53 57 49 50; www.hroosevelt.com 🚇 Franklin-D Roosevelt

Hôtel du Jeu de Paume (€€€)

Exclusive hotel on the Île Saint-Louis, housed in converted Jeu de Paume (inside tennis court), with striking galleries and mezzanines.

✉ 54 rue Saint-Louis-en-l'Île, 75004 ☎ 01 43 26 14 18; www.hoteljeudepaume.com 🚇 Pont-Marie

Hôtel Meurice (€€€)

The luxurious bedrooms at the Hotel Meurice, overlooking the Jardin des Tuileries, have antique furniture and original paintings.

✉ 228 rue de Rivoli, 75001 ☎ 01 44 58 10 10; www.hotelmeurice.com 🚇 Tuileries

Hôtel Montalembert (€€€)

Luxury hotel, with discreet yet original decoration, sound-proofing and air-conditioning; a quality hotel at top prices.

✉ 3 rue de Montalembert, 75007 ☎ 01 45 49 68 68; www.montalembert.com 🕙 All year 🚇 Rue du Bac

Hôtel du Panthéon (€€)

An elegant hotel conveniently situated in the university district, with well-appointed air-conditioned bedrooms.

✉ 19 place du Panthéon, 75005 ☎ 01 43 54 32 95; www.hoteldupantheon.com 🕙 All year 🚇 Cardinal-Lemoine

Hôtel Place des Vosges (€)

Picturesque, quiet hotel just off the place des Vosges.

✉ 12 rue de Birague, 75004 ☎ 01 42 72 60 46 🕙 All year 🚇 Saint-Paul, Bastille

Hôtel Ritz Paris (€€€)

Sometimes called the palace of kings and the king of palaces, the Ritz shares with the Crillon the top of the list of Paris's luxury hotels. Overlooking the place Vendôme, it has a beautiful swimming pool and luxury fitness centre; prices are accordingly very high.

✉ 15 place Vendôme, 75001 ☎ 01 43 16 45 33; www.ritzparis.com 🕙 All year 🚇 Opéra

Best shopping

Au Printemps
Three stores in one: Le Printemps de la Mode, including ready-to-wear designer fashion; Le Printemps de la Maison, including elegant tableware and hi-fi, record and stationery department in the basement; and Brummell, devoted to menswear.
✉ 64 boulevard Haussmann, 75009 ☎ 01 42 82 50 00 Ⓜ Havre-Caumartin

Boulangerie Poîlane
The most famous bakery in Paris. Long queues form outside this shop for the traditionally baked bread.
✉ 8 rue du Cherche-Midi, 75006 ☎ 01 45 48 42 59 Ⓜ Sèvres-Babylone

Carrousel du Louvre
Elegant shopping centre beneath the place du Carrousel and connecting with the Louvre; several boutiques connected with the arts, Virgin store and a number of bars serving food from different countries.
✉ 99 rue de Rivoli, 75001 ☎ 01 43 16 47 47 Ⓜ Palais Royal

Fauchon and Hédiard
Strictly for gourmets! Two delicatessen shops with high-quality French regional products.
✉ Fauchon at No 26, Hédiard at No 21 place de la Madeleine, 75008
☎ Fauchon: 01 47 42 91 10; Hédiard: 01 43 12 88 88 Ⓜ Madeleine

FNAC
Books, hi-fi, videos, CDs, cameras, computers, on several floors.
✉ 6 avenue des Ternes, 75017 (other branches in Montparnasse, Les Halles and Bastille) ☎ 01 44 09 18 00 Ⓜ Ternes

Galeries Lafayette

A few blocks from Au Printemps, with designer ready-to-wear fashion and lingerie. Under a giant glass dome is an enticing display of everything a home and its inhabitants need.

✉ 40 boulevard Haussmann, 75009 ☎ 01 42 82 34 56 🚇 Chaussée d'Antin

Jean-Paul Gaultier

Ready-to-wear fashion from this famous designer.

✉ 30 rue du Faubourg Saint-Antoine, 75012 ☎ 01 44 68 84 84 🚇 Bastille

Louvre des Antiquaires

This centre houses around 250 classy antique shops on three floors.

✉ 2 place du Palais-Royal, 75001 ☎ 01 42 97 27 27 🚇 Palais-Royal

Marché Saint-Germain

Fashion and gift shops including clothes, shoes, leather goods, accessories, perfume, jewellery and gifts.

✉ Rue Clément, 75006 🚇 Mabillon

Shakespeare & Company

New and second-hand books in English.

✉ 37 rue de la Bûcherie, 75005 ☎ 01 43 26 96 50 🚇 Maubert-Mutualité

Exploring

The city of Paris has always played its role of capital of France to the full. It is where the French nation's future is decided, where revolutions began in the past and where major political, economic and social changes are traditionally launched. This is as true today as it ever was, in spite of many attempts at decentralization.

Parisian life reflects the city's leading role in many different ways: the numerous trade exhibitions and international conferences taking place every year testify to its economic and potitical dynamism and healthy competitive spirit. Paris is continually on the move in all fields of human activity: its architectural heritage is constantly expanding and it is proudly setting new trends in the arts, in gastronomy and in fashion. Paris is also a cosmopolitan metropolis where many ethnic groups find the necessary scope to express their differences.

The Latin Quarter and the Islands

Situated on the Left Bank between the Carrefour de l'Odéon and the Jardin des Plantes, the lively Latin Quarter was known in medieval times as the 'Montagne Ste-Geneviève' after the patron saint of Paris, and was later given the name of 'Quartier Latin' because Latin was spoken at the university until the late 18th century. To this day it remains the undisputed kingdom of Parisian students. The Sorbonne, the most famous French university

college, was founded in 1257; the present building dates from the late 19th century when well-known artists such as Puvis de Chavannes decorated the interior. The adjacent 17th-century church is a model of Jesuit style.

The two river islands – Île de la Cité and Île St-Louis – have very different histories and characters. The Ile de la Cité is not only the historic centre of Paris, it is also a place of exceptional natural beauty and home to three major monuments – Notre-Dame, Sainte-Chapelle and the Conciergerie. The peaceful atmosphere of the Île St-Louis is apparent as soon as you walk along its shaded embankment, lined with elegant 17th-century mansions that stand as silent witnesses of a bygone era.

CITÉ, ÎLE DE LA

The Celtic tribe the Parisii settled on the largest island in an area known as Lutetia, which under the Romans expanded onto the Left Bank of the Seine. Nevertheless, the island (the Cité), which the king of the Franks chose as his capital in AD 508, remained for 1,000 years the seat of royal, judicial and religious power. During the Middle Ages, the Île de la Cité was an important intellectual centre as its cathedral schools attracted students from all over Europe. Even after the kings of France left the royal palace for larger premises on the Right Bank, the Cité lost none of its symbolic importance and remains to this day the 'guardian' of 2,000 years of history.

The appearance of the Cité has changed considerably over the years; in the 19th century, the centre of the island was cleared and the vast square in front of Notre-Dame Cathedral created. At the other end of the island, the Conciergerie and Sainte-Chapelle are the only remaining parts of the medieval royal palace, now incorporated in the huge Palais de Justice.

🚇 20L ✉ Île de la Cité, 75001 and 75004 🍴 Restaurants and cafés (€–€€) on the island and on the Right and Left banks 🚇 Cité, Pont Neuf, St-Michel, Châtelet, Hôtel de Ville 🚌 21, 24, 27, 38, 47, 58, 70, 85, 96

LA CONCIERGERIE

For most people, the name 'Conciergerie' suggests crowds of innocent prisoners waiting to be taken to the guillotine. Nowadays, its familiar round towers covered with conical slate roofs and the square clock tower, which housed the first public clock in Paris, are one of the most picturesque sights of the Île de la Cité. The Conciergerie is the last remaining authentic part of a 14th-century royal complex, administered by a *concierge* or governor. The twin towers marked the main entrance to the palace. In the late 14th century, the Conciergerie was turned into a prison but it only acquired a sinister connotation during the Revolution, when it held a number of famous prisoners, including Queen Marie-Antoinette, Madame du Barry and the poet André Chénier, as well as Danton and Robespierre. The visit includes the original guards' room, a magnificent great hall with Gothic vaulting and kitchens with monumental fireplaces. There is also a reconstruction of Marie-Antoinette's cell.

🚇 20L ✉ 2 boulevard du Palais, 75001 ☎ 01 53 73 78 50 🕐 Daily 9.30–6. Closed 1 Jan, 1 May, 25 Dec ✋ Moderate 🚇 Cité, Châtelet 🚌 21, 24, 27, 38, 58, 85, 81, 85, 96, Balabus ❓ Guided tours, bookshop

GOBELINS, MANUFACTURE NATIONALE DES

The former royal tapestry factory, founded by Colbert in 1664 to make beautiful tapestries for the royal household, is still going strong. Priceless works of art, based on paintings by artists such as Le Brun and Boucher and, more recently, Lurçat and Picasso, have been produced in the workshops over the last three centuries. Techniques have hardly changed since the 17th century and looms are either upright (*haute lice* method) or horizontal (*basse lice* method). The 17th-century buildings also house the Savonnerie carpet factory, founded in 1604, and the Beauvais tapestry factory, founded at the same time as the Gobelins.

21G (off map) ✉ 42 avenue des Gobelins, 75013 ☎ 01 44 54 19 33; 01 44 08 52 00 🕐 Tue, Wed, Thu guided tours only at 2 and 2.45. Closed public hols 🖐 Moderate 🚇 Les Gobelins 🚌 27, 47, 83, 91

INSTITUT DU MONDE ARABE

The Institute of Arab and Islamic Civilization is a remarkable piece of modern architecture designed by the French architect Jean Nouvel. Its glass-and-aluminium façade, reminiscent of a *musharabia* (carved wooden screen), discretely refers to Arab tradition. The seventh floor houses a museum of Islamic art and civilization from the 8th century to the present day. The ninth floor offers a panoramic view of the Île de la Cité and Île St-Louis near by.

22J ✉ 1 rue des Fossés St-Bernard, 75005 ☎ 01 40 51 38 38 🕐 Tue–Sun 10–6. Closed 1 May 🖐 Inexpensive 🍴 Restaurant (€–€€) 🚇 Jussieu 🚌 24, 63, 67, 86, 87, 89 ❓ Guided tours, shops

ENTRÉE
EXPOSITION

ENTRÉE
PRINCIPALE

MOYEN-AGE, MUSÉE NATIONAL DU

This museum, also known as the Musée de Cluny (➤ 75), stands at the heart of the Quartier Latin, on the site of Gallo-Roman baths dating from the 3rd century AD. The ruins are surrounded by a public garden. Inside the main courtyard, the elegant stair tower and corner turrets are particularly noteworthy. All the arts and crafts of the medieval period are illustrated, the most famous exhibit being a set of tapestries known as 'La Dame à la Licorne', made in a Brussels workshop at the end of the 15th century. There is also an exceptionally fine collection of sculptures, including the heads of the kings of Judaea that decorated the façade of Notre-Dame Cathedral and were knocked down during the Revolution.

www.musee-moyenage.fr

✚ 20K ✉ 6 place Paul Painlevé, 75005 ☎ 01 53 73 78 00; 01 53 73 78 16 ⏰ Wed–Mon 9.15–5.45. Closed 1 Jan, 1 May, 25 Dec ✋ Inexpensive 🍴 Boulevard St-Michel nearby (€–€€) 🚇 Cluny-La Sorbonne 🚌 21, 27, 38, 63, 85, 86, 87 ❓ Guided tours, shops, concerts

NOTRE-DAME

See pages 46–47.

PANTHÉON

Commissioned by Louis XV, the building was meant to replace St Genevieve's Church in the Quartier Latin; designed by Soufflot, who gave it the shape of a Greek cross surmounted by a high dome, it is now one of Paris's landmarks. Completed on the eve of the Revolution, it became a Pantheon for France's illustrious dead, among them Voltaire, Rousseau, Hugo, Zola, and more recently Jean Moulin (head of the French Resistance during World War II) and André Malraux (writer and highly successful Minister of Culture).

✚ 20J ✉ Place du Panthéon, 75005 ☎ 01 44 32 18 00 ⏰ Apr–Sep daily 10–6.30; Oct–Mar daily 10–6. Closed 1 Jan, 1 May, 25 Dec ✋ Moderate 🚇 Cardinal-Lemoine 🚌 84, 89 ❓ Shops

VIVRE LIBRE OU MOURIR

LA CONVENTION NATIONALE

PLANTES, JARDIN DES

The botanical gardens owe their name to the 'royal garden of medicinal plants' created in the 17th century. Today they form the experimental gardens of the Musée National d'Histoire Naturelle (Natural History Museum) and make an ideal spot for a leisurely stroll; children love the *ménagerie* (zoo). There are also hothouses, an alpine garden and several exhibition halls, the most fascinating being the Grande Galerie de l'Evolution, illustrating the evolution of life on earth and Man's influence on it. Here, the display of endangered and extinct species is particularly interesting. Also featured are the scientists closely associated with evolution and the latest discoveries in the field of genetics.

🛨 22H ✉ 57 rue Cuvier, 75005 ☎ 01 40 79 30 00 ⊛ Gardens: daily 7.30–sunset. Museum: Wed–Mon 10–5. Zoo: daily 9–6 ✋ Gardens: free; museum and zoo: moderate 🍴 Cafeteria (€) 🚇 Jussieu ❓ Lectures, exhibitions, workshops for children, shop

LES QUAIS

See pages 50–51.

ST-ETIENNE-DU-MONT

The Church of St-Etienne-du-Mont, dating from the late 15th century, combines Flamboyant Gothic and Renaissance styles. Don't miss the delicately fretted rood-screen inside.

🛨 20J ✉ Place Ste-Geneviève, 75005 ⊛ Jul–Aug Tue–Sun 10–12, 4–7.15; Sep–Jun Mon–Sat 8.30–12, 2–7.15 ✋ Free 🚇 Cardinal Lemoine 🚌 84, 89

SAINTE-CHAPELLE

The full splendour of this magnificent Gothic chapel, surely Paris's most beautiful church, can only be appreciated from inside, as Sainte-Chapelle is unfortunately closely surrounded by the Palais de Justice buildings. Commissioned by Louis IX, a king so devout that he came to be known as Saint Louis, to house the Crown of Thorns and a fragment of the true Cross, it was built in less than three years by Pierre de Montreuil (who also worked on Notre-Dame) and was consecrated in 1248.

The building consists of two chapels, the lower one intended as a parish church for the palace staff and the upper one reserved for the royal family. The latter is a striking example of technical prowess: walls have been replaced by 15m-high (49ft) stained-glass panels linked by slender pillars which also support the vaulting. The stained-glass windows, which cover an area of more than 600sq m (6,460sq ft), are mainly original and illustrate scenes from the Old and New Testaments.

➕ 20L ✉ 4 boulevard du Palais, 75001 ☎ 01 53 40 60 80 🕐 Oct–Mar daily 10–5; Apr–Sep daily 9.30–6.30. Closed 1 Jan, 1 May, 1 Nov 💰 Moderate 🚇 Cité 🚌 96 ❓ Shop

ST-LOUIS, ÎLE

The island was formed at the beginning of the 17th century, when two small islands were united and joined to the mainland by a couple of bridges linked by the rue des Deux Ponts, which still exists; at the same time, private residences were built along the embankment and the straight narrow streets. The whole project was completed in a remarkably short time between 1627 and 1664. Since then, time seems to have stood still on the Île Saint-Louis, which to this day retains its provincial character.

A few architectural gems can be seen along quai de Bourbon and quai d'Anjou, which offer fine views of the Right Bank. From the western tip of the island you can see Notre-Dame and the Île de la Cité. Concerts are regularly given in the Classical Church of St-Louis-en-l'Île, richly decorated inside.

➕ 22K ✉ 75004 🍴 Rue St-Louis-en-l'Île (€€) 🚇 Pont Marie 🚌 67, 86, 87

ST-SÉVERIN

St-Séverin is one of the most beautiful churches in the capital, with its delightful blend of Flamboyant Gothic architecture and contemporary stained glass. It dates originally from the 13th century and is dedicated to the 6th-century hermit St Séverin, who was closely associated with St Martin, patron saint of travellers. The surrounding cobbled streets, full of cafés, shops and cheap eateries, are popular with students and visitors alike.

www.saint-severin.com

➕ 20K ✉ 1 rue des Prêtres-St-Séverin, 75005 ☎ 01 42 34 93 50
🕐 Mon–Sat 11–7.30, Sun 9–8.30 🚇 Saint-Michel

HOTELS

Hôtel Esmeralda (€€)
Some rooms in this old-fashioned yet cosy hotel offer delightful views of Notre-Dame. Beware – no lift!
✉ 4 rue Saint-Julien-le-Pauvre, 75005 ☎ 01 43 54 19 20 🚇 Saint-Michel

Hôtel des Grandes Écoles (€€)
This delightful oasis of peace in the Latin Quarter has its own garden. Rooms are decorated in elegant country style.
✉ 75 rue Cardinal-Lemoine, 75005 ☎ 01 43 26 79 23; www.hotel-grandes-ecoles.com 🚇 Cardinal-Lemoine, Place Monge

Hôtel du Jeu de Paume (€€€)
See page 78.

Hôtel du Lys (€)
Simple hotel at the heart of the Quartier Latin; no lift but modern bathrooms, warm welcome and reasonable prices; book well in advance.
✉ 23 rue Serpente, 75006 ☎ 01 43 26 97 57 🚇 Saint-Michel, Odéon

Hôtel du Panthéon (€€)
See page 79.

Relais St-Jacques (€€€)
This small hotel offers 23 comfortable, individually styled rooms, close to the Luxembourg Gardens.
✉ 3 rue de l'Abbé de l'Epée, 75005 ☎ 01 53 73 26 00 🚇 Luxembourg

Résidence les Gobelins (€€)
A haven of peace near the lively rue Mouffetard; warm welcome.
✉ 9 rue des Gobelins, 75013 ☎ 01 47 07 26 90; www.hotelgobelins.com
🚇 Les Gobelins

Hôtel Les Rives de Notre-Dame (€€€)

Elegant and comfortable, with soundproofed bedrooms overlooking the quai Saint-Michel and the Île de la Cité.

✉ 15 quai Saint-Michel, 75005 ☎ 01 43 54 81 16; www.rivesdenotredame.com 🚇 Saint-Michel

Select Hôtel (€€)

Fully modernized hotel in the heart of the Latin Quarter, close to the Luxembourg gardens; intimate atmosphere; glass-roofed patio.

✉ 1 place de la Sorbonne, 75005 ☎ 01 46 34 14 80; www.selecthotel.fr 🚇 Cluny-la-Sorbonne, Odéon

Hôtel des Trois Collèges (€)

Roof beams and dormer windows add a picturesque touch to this simple yet comfortable hotel close to the Sorbonne.

✉ 16 rue Cujas, 75005 ☎ 01 43 54 67 30; www.3colleges.com 🚇 Cluny-la-Sorbonne

RESTAURANTS

Brasserie Balzar (€€)

Popular smart brasserie close to the Sorbonne, serving good French dishes.

✉ 49 rue des Écoles, 75005 ☎ 01 43 54 13 67; www.brasseriebalzar.com 🕐 Daily 🚇 Cluny-La Sorbonne

La Criée (€)

For lovers of seafood at affordable prices!

✉ 15 rue Lagrange, 75005 ☎ 01 43 54 23 57; www.lacriee.com 🕐 Lunch, dinner 🚇 Maubert–Mutualité

Mavrommatis (€–€€)

Refined traditional Greek cuisine; alfresco dining on the terrace in summer.

✉ 5 rue du Marché des Patriarches, 75005 ☎ 01 43 31 17 17; www.mavromatis.fr 🕐 Lunch, dinner; closed Mon 🚇 Censier-Daubenton

Mon Vieil Ami (€€)

Trendy rustic décor; delicious, reasonably priced dishes.

✉ 69 rue Saint-Louis-en-l'Ile, 75004 ☎ 01 40 46 01 35 🕐 Lunch, dinner; closed Mon and Tue lunch 🚇 Pont-Marie

Nos Ancêtres les Gaulois (€€)

Convivial atmosphere; menu includes as much wine as you can drink.

✉ 39 rue St-Louis-en-l'Ile, 75004 ☎ 01 46 33 66 07; www.nosancetreslesgaulois.com 🕐 Dinner only, lunch on Sun 🚇 Pont-Marie

La Parcheminerie (€–€€)

Delightful bistro in picturesque pedestrian street of the Latin Quarter.

✉ 31 rue de la Parcheminerie, 75005 ☎ 01 46 33 65 12 🕐 Lunch, dinner; closed Sun and Mon 🚇 Saint-Michel

Le Reminet (€–€€)

Refined bistro-style fare; terrace in summer. Extraordinarily good desserts. Friendly service.

✉ 3 rue des Grands-Degrés, 75005 ☎ 01 44 07 04 24 🕐 Lunch, dinner; closed Mon, Tue, 1–21 Jan and 15–31 Aug 🚇 Saint-Michel

Susan's Place (€)

Convivial Tex-Mex restaurant also serving vegetarian dishes.

✉ 51 rue des Écoles, 75005 ☎ 01 43 54 23 22 🕐 Lunch, dinner; closed Sun lunch, Mon 🚇 Maubert-Mutualité

La Tour d'Argent (€€€)

See page 63.

La Truffière (€€)

Very refined cuisine served in pleasant surroundings. The menu makes good use of truffles, as the name suggests.

✉ 4 rue Blainville, 75005 ☎ 01 46 33 29 82 🕐 Lunch, dinner; closed Mon 🚇 Place Monge

SHOPPING

ART, ANTIQUES AND HANDICRAFTS
La Tuile à Loup
Handicrafts from various French regions.
✉ 35 rue Daubenton, 75005 ☎ 01 47 07 28 90; www.latuilealoup.com
🚇 Censier-Daubenton

BOOKS, CDs, VIDEOS AND HI-FI
The Abbey Bookshop
New and second-hand books from Britain, Canada and the USA.
✉ 29 rue de la Parcheminerie, 75005 ☎ 01 46 33 16 24 🚇 Saint-Michel

Librairie Gourmand
Books on the history of food, culinary antiques, drawings and
lithographs.
✉ 4 rue Dante, 75005 ☎ 01 43 54 37 27 🚇 Saint-Michel

Librairie Ulysse
New and second-hand books, maps and magazines from around
the world in a congenial atmosphere.
✉ 26 rue St-Louis en l'Île, 75004 ☎ 01 43 25 17 35; www.ulysse.fr
🚇 Sully Morland

Shakespeare & Company
See page 81.

FOOD AND WINES
Berthillon
Mouth-watering ice cream in a wide range of flavours.
✉ 31 rue Saint-Louis-en-l'Île, 75004 ☎ 01 43 54 31 61 🕐 Closed Mon
and Tue 🚇 Pont-Marie

La Ferme St-Aubin
Delicious French and European cheeses, all in peak condition.
✉ 76 rue Saint-Louis-en-l'Île, 75004 ☎ 01 43 54 74 54 🕐 Closed Mon
🚇 Pont-Marie

MARKETS
Marché aux Fleurs
Picturesque daily market (8–7) that becomes a bird market on Sundays (8–7).
✉ Place Louis Lépine, Île de la Cité, 75004 🚇 Cité

Marché de la rue Mouffetard
Superb selection of fruit and vegetables, cheese and *charcuterie* (deli), Tuesdays, Thursdays and Saturdays.
✉ Rue Mouffetard, 75005 🚇 Monge

ENTERTAINMENT

CABARET
Paradis Latin
Dinner followed by a live cabaret.
✉ 28 rue du Cardinal Lemoine, 75005 ☎ 01 43 25 28 28; www.paradis-latin.com 🕐 Closed Tue 🚇 Cardinal Lemoine

CINEMA
Studio Galande
Shows such cult offerings as *The Rocky Horror Show* Fridays and Saturdays, with art films and cartoons the rest of the week.
✉ 42 rue Galande, 75005 ☎ 01 43 26 94 08; www.studiogalande.fr
🚇 Saint-Michel

DANCE CLUB
Le Saint
Small dance club offering a wide range of music to suit most tastes.
✉ 7 rue St-Séverin, 75005 ☎ 01 40 20 43 23; www.lesaintdisco.com
🚇 Saint-Michel

JAZZ CLUBS
Caveau de la Huchette
See page 73.

Le Petit Journal
Traditional jazz from top-class performers.
✉ 71 boulevard St-Michel, 75005 ☎ 01 43 26 28 59 🚇 Luxembourg,
Saint-Michel

NIGHTCLUBS AND BARS
Le Mambo Club
Exotic décor, Afro music, salsa…
✉ 20 rue Cujas, 75005 ☎ 01 43 54 89 21 🚇 Luxembourg

Piano Vache
A well-established venue where you can enjoy acoustic music
over a draught beer.
✉ 8 rue Laplace, 75005 ☎ 01 46 33 75 03 🚇 Maubert-Mutalité

Zed Club
Rock, jazz, swing, salsa and 1960s–1990s pop.
✉ 2 rue des Anglais, 75005 ☎ 01 43 54 93 78 🚇 Maubert-Mutalité

SPORT
Piscine Pontoise Quartier Latin
Fitness club with swimming pool, squash court, sauna.
✉ 19 rue de Pontoise, 75005 ☎ 01 55 42 77 88 🚇 Maubert-Mutualité

THEATRE
Théâtre de la Huchette
A Parisian institution, with performances of masterpieces by
Ionesco.
✉ 23 rue de la Huchette, 75005 ☎ 01 43 26 38 99 🚇 Saint-Michel

Eiffel Tower to St-Germain-des-Prés

The Rive Gauche (Left Bank), with its narrow streets lined with shops and restaurants, and its breathtaking monuments, exudes Parisian charm. It's one of the most sought-after residential districts in Paris and eternally magnetic to both visitors and residents.

The Left Bank in this chapter comprises the area from the Tour Eiffel in the west to the Jardin du Luxembourg in the east, and south to include Montparnasse, popular with artists and writers in the early 20th century. Some of the city's best-known attractions are found here – the Musée d'Orsay, housed in a magnificent Industrial Age train terminus, the atmospheric Quartier St-Germain-des-Prés, with its literary associations, the imposing architectural ensemble of Les Invalides, and that marvel of 19th-century engineering, the Eiffel Tower.

ASSEMBLÉE NATIONALE PALAIS-BOURBON

The façade of this neoclassical building, housing the lower house of the French parliament, echoes that of the Madeleine across the place de la Concorde. Completed by Louis XV's famous architect Gabriel, the Palais-Bourbon still bears the name of the French royal family to whom it once belonged. Guided tours (identity document required) include the chamber, where members of parliament sit on benches arranged in semicircular tiers, several reception rooms and the library, richly decorated by Delacroix.

➕ 6B ✉ 33 quai d'Orsay, 75007 ☎ 01 40 63 60 08
🕐 Guided tours only Sat 10am, 2pm, 3pm. Closed public hols and when Parliament is sitting ♿ Free 🚇 Assemblée Nationale 🚌 63, 83, 84, 94 🛍 Shops

EUGÈNE DELACROIX, MUSÉE NATIONAL

The old-world charm of the tiny rue de Furstenberg, hidden behind the Church of St-Germain-des-Prés, is the perfect setting for a museum devoted to one of the major French Romantic painters. Delacroix lived and worked here until the end of his life and, besides a few paintings, the place is full of mementoes of the artist, letters, sketches...and his palette. There is also a bookshop. It is well worth taking time to explore the picturesque neighbourhood and the open market in rue de Buci.
www.musee-delacroix.fr

➕ 18L ✉ 6 rue de Furstenberg, 75006 ☎ 01 44 41 86 50
🕐 Wed–Mon 9.30–5. Closed public hols ♿ Inexpensive
🚇 St-Germain-des-Prés 🚌 39, 48, 63, 95

FAUBOURG ST-GERMAIN

This 'suburb' is today one of the most elegant districts of central Paris. Its name came from the nearby Abbaye de St-Germain-des-Prés to which it belonged in medieval times. University students loved to stroll through the meadows stretching down to the river west of the abbey and the area remained in its natural state until the 18th century, when it became fashionable for the aristocracy and the wealthy middle class to have mansions built there by the famous architects of the time.

The rue de Varenne is lined with the famous Hôtel Matignon, now the prime minister's residence, and the Hôtel Biron, better known as the Musée Rodin (➤ 109). The parallel rue de Grenelle is interesting for its wealth of authentic architecture, including the Hôtel de Villars, now the town hall of the 7th *arrondissement*. Further along, on the opposite side, is an interesting museum (No 59) devoted to the sculptor Maillol (➤ 106).

✚ 18L ✉ 75007 ⏱ For the museums' opening times, see the relevant entries 🍴 Cafés and restaurants nearby in boulevard St-Germain (€–€€) Ⓜ Varenne, Rue du Bac 🚌 69, 83, 84, 94

INSTITUT DE FRANCE

The imposing Classical building facing the Louvre across the river was commissioned by Cardinal Mazarin as a school for provincial children, and designed by Le Vau; it is topped by a magnificent dome and houses the Institut de France, created in 1795 to unite under one roof five prestigious academies, including the Académie Française, founded in 1635 by Richelieu. It also houses the Bibliothèque Mazarine, Mazarin's own collection of rare editions.

✚ 18L ✉ 23 quai de Conti, 75006 ☎ 01 44 41 44 35 ⏱ Sat, Sun guided tours by appointment only ✋ Inexpensive Ⓜ Pont Neuf, Louvre, Odéon 🚌 24, 27, 39, 48, 58, 70, 95

LES INVALIDES

See pages 42–43.

LUXEMBOURG, JARDIN DU

Just a stone's throw from the Sorbonne, this attractive French-style garden is traditionally the haunt of students and lovers, who particularly favour the area surrounding the Fontaine de Médicis, named after Marie de Médicis, who commissioned the Palais du Luxembourg (now the Senate) and the gardens.

🚩 18J ✉ Boulevard St-Michel, 75006 ☎ 01 42 34 23 62 🕐 Apr–Oct daily 7am–7.30pm; Mar and Nov daily 8–dusk 🚇 Luxembourg

MAILLOL, MUSÉE

This atttractive museum, in the rue de Grenelle next to a beautiful 18th-century fountain, is interesting on two accounts: it displays a great many works by the French painter and sculptor Aristide Maillol (1861–1944), as well as a private collection of works by Ingres, Cézanne, Dufy, Matisse, Bonnard, Degas, Picasso, Gauguin, Rodin, Kandinsky and Poliakoff among others. Maillol's obsessive theme was the nude, upon which he conferred an allegorical meaning; he produced smooth rounded figures, some of which can be seen in the Jardin des Tuileries.

🚩 16L ✉ 61 rue de Grenelle, 75007 ☎ 01 42 22 59 58 🕐 Wed–Mon 11–6. Closed public hols 🖐 Moderate 🍴 Cafeteria (€) 🚇 Rue du Bac 🚌 63, 68, 69, 83, 84 🛈 Shop

MONTPARNASSE

Fashions change quickly in artistic circles and, soon after the turn of the 20th century, young artists and writers left Montmartre to settle on the Left Bank, in an area which had been known as Montparnasse since medieval times. Modigliani, Chagall, Léger and many others found studios in La Ruche, the counterpart of the Bateau-Lavoir in Montmartre (➤ 154). They were later joined by

Russian political refugees, musicians and, between the wars, American writers of the 'lost generation', among them Hemingway. They met in cafés along boulevard Montparnasse, which have since become household names: La Closerie des Lilas, La Rotonde, Le Select, La Coupole and Le Dôme.

Since the 1960s the district has been modernized and a new business complex built south of the boulevard. The 200m-high (656ft) **Tour Montparnasse** stands in front of one of the busiest stations in Paris. The tower's 56th and 59th floors are open to the public and offer a restaurant and panoramic views.

🚌 16G ✉ 75014 🚇 Montparnasse-Bienvenüe, Vavin

Tour Montparnasse

✉ Rue de l'Arrivée, 75015 ☎ 01 45 38 52 56 🕐 Daily 9.30am–10.30pm (11.30pm in summer) 💷 Moderate 🍴 Le Ciel de Paris (€€)

ORSAY, MUSÉE D'

See pages 48–49.

RODIN, MUSÉE

Rodin spent the last few years of his life in the Hôtel Biron as a guest of the French nation; when he died the collection of his works reverted to the State and the mansion was turned into a museum. His forceful and highly original style brought him many disappointments and failures: his *Man with a Broken Nose* (now in the museum) was refused at the 1864 Salon and Rodin had to wait for another 15 years before his talent was fully acknowledged through his *St John the Baptist*. His major works are inside the museum *(The Kiss, Man Walking)* and in the gardens *(The Thinker, The Burghers of Calais, The Gates of Hell)*.

www.musee-rodin.fr

➕ 15L ✉ 77 rue de Varenne, 75007 ☎ 01 44 18 61 10 🕐 Tue–Sun 9.30–4.45 (5.45 in summer, park 6.45). Closed 1 Jan, 25 Dec ✋ Inexpensive 🍴 Cafeteria (€) 🚇 Varenne, Invalides, Saint-François-Xavier 🚌 69, 82, 87, 92 ❓ Guided tours, shops

ST-GERMAIN-DES-PRÉS

The Benedictine Abbey of St-Germain-des-Prés, founded in the 6th century, was throughout the Middle Ages so powerful a religious and cultural centre that it became a town within the town. It was completely destroyed during the Revolution; only the church was spared. In spite of many alterations, the church is a fine example of Romanesque style: the tower dates from the 11th century as does the nave; note that the carved capitals on the pillars are copies of the originals kept in the Musée National du Moyen-Âge (➤ 90). The chancel and ambulatory date from the 12th century.

It is worth exploring the old streets on the north and east sides of the church and strolling along boulevard St-Germain. The area between boulevard St-Germain and the river and between rue du Bac and rue de Seine is full of antique shops and art galleries.

➕ 18L ✉ Place St-Germain-des-Prés, 75006 ☎ 01 55 42 81 33 🕐 Daily 8–7 ✋ Free 🍴 Cafés/restaurants near by (€–€€) 🚇 St-Germain-des-Prés

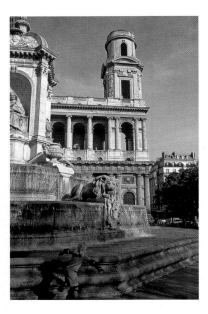

ST-SULPICE

The original church, founded by the Abbey of St-Germain-des-Prés, was rebuilt and extended in the 17th century but was not completed until the mid-18th century. The Italian-style façade, designed by Servandoni, is surmounted by two slightly different towers crowned by balustrades and is in marked contrast to the rest of the building. Among the wealth of interior decoration are several statues by Bouchardon and outstanding murals by Delacroix (first chapel on the right) as well as a splendid organ by Cavaillé-Coll, traditionally played by the best organists in France. Servandoni had also submitted plans for the square in front of the church, but they were abandoned and a monumental fountain designed by Visconti was eventually placed in its centre in 1844.

✠ 18K ✉ Place St-Sulpice, 75006 ☎ 01 46 33 21 78 🕐 Daily 7.30–7.30 👆 Free 🚇 St-Sulpice

LA TOUR EIFFEL

See pages 52–53.

HOTELS

Hôtel de l'Abbaye (€€€)

A roaring log fire and a delightful inner garden ensure comfort whatever the season.

✉ 10 rue Cassette, 75006 ☎ 01 45 44 38 11; www.hotel-abbaye.com
🚇 Rennes

Hôtel d'Angleterre Saint-Germain-des-Prés (€€–€€€)

See page 78.

Hôtel du Lys (€)

Simple hotel at the heart of the Quartier Latin; no elevator but modern bathrooms, warm welcome and reasonable prices; make reservations well in advance.

✉ 23 rue Serpente, 75006 ☎ 01 43 26 97 57 🚇 Saint-Michel, Odéon

Hôtel Montalembert (€€€)

See page 79.

Hôtel de Nevers (€)

Simple but charming, in a former convent building; private roof terraces for top-floor rooms.

✉ 83 rue du Bac, 75007 ☎ 01 45 44 61 30 🚇 Rue du Bac

Hôtel Le Régent (€€)

Air-conditioning and bright well-appointed bedrooms in this cleverly restored 18th-century house in St-Germain-des-Prés.

✉ 61 rue Dauphine, 75006 ☎ 01 46 34 59 80 🚇 Odéon

Hôtel Le Tourville (€€–€€€)

Refined decoration for this modern hotel in the elegant 7th *arrondissement*, close to Les Invalides.

✉ 16 avenue de Tourville, 75007 ☎ 01 47 05 62 62; www.tourville.com
🚇 Ecole Militaire

RESTAURANTS

Bistrot du 7e (€)
Attractive bistro near les Invalides, excellent value for money.
✉ 56 boulevard de la Tour-Maubourg, 75007 ☎ 01 45 51 93 08 🕓 Lunch,
dinner; closed Sat and Sun lunch 🚇 Invalides, La Tour-Maubourg

Les Bookinistes (€€)
Fashionable restaurant along the embankment; up-and-coming
young chef has made nouvelle cuisine into an art.
✉ 53 quai des Grands-Augustins, 75006 ☎ 01 43 25 45 94 🕓 Lunch, dinner;
closed Sat and Sun lunch 🚇 Saint-Michel

Brasserie Lipp (€€)
See page 62.

Le Ciel de Paris (€€–€€€)
On the 56th floor of the Tour Montparnasse; live music from 9pm.
✉ Tour Montparnasse, 33 avenue du Maine, 75015 ☎ 01 40 64 77 69;
www.cieldeparis.com 🕓 Lunch, dinner 🚇 Montparnasse-Bienvenüe

D'Chez Eux (€€)
Bistro specializing in cassoulet (haricot-bean stew with Toulouse
sausages). Terrace.
✉ 2 avenue Lowendal, 75007 ☎ 01 47 05 52 55; www.chezeux.com
🕓 Lunch, dinner; closed Sun and first 3 weeks of Aug 🚇 Ecole Militaire

Côté Seine (€–€€)
Along the embankment between Notre-Dame and the pont Neuf.
Good value for money; book ahead.
✉ 45 quai des Grands-Augustins, 75006 ☎ 01 43 54 49 73 🕓 Dinner
🚇 Saint-Michel

La Coupole (€€)
See page 62.

Le Divellec (€€€)
See page 62.

Le Dôme (€€–€€€)

Brasserie specializing in all types of seafood. Especially good is the bouillabaisse from Provence.

✉ 108 boulevard du Montparnasse, 75014 ☎ 01 43 35 34 82 🕐 Lunch, dinner 🚇 Vavin

L'Epi Dupin (€)

Sought-after, reasonably priced restaurant with regular change of menu; book well in advance. Best ingredients from Rungis market. Terrace.

✉ 11 rue Dupin, 75006 ☎ 01 42 22 64 56 🕐 Lunch, dinner; closed Sat, Sun and Mon lunch and first 3 weeks in Aug 🚇 Sèvres-Babylone

La Frégate (€–€€)

Next to the Musée d'Orsay and facing the Louvre; good-value traditional French cuisine.

✉ 1 rue de Bac, 75007 ☎ 01 42 61 23 77 🕐 Lunch, dinner 🚇 Rue de Bac

Jacques Cagna (€€€)

See page 63.

Le Polidor (€)

See page 60.

Le Procope (€–€€)

An 18th-century literary café known to Voltaire and Benjamin Franklin, now a historic monument.

✉ 13 rue de l'Ancienne Comédie, 75006 ☎ 01 40 46 79 00; www.procope.com 🕐 Lunch, dinner 🚇 Odéon

La Régalade (€–€€)

Haute cuisine at relatively low prices in an unassuming setting; book well in advance.

✉ 49 avenue Jean Moulin, 75014 ☎ 01 45 45 68 58 🕐 Lunch, dinner; closed Sun and Mon lunch 🚇 Alesia

Thoumieux (€–€€)

High-class brasserie specializing in home-made duck cassoulet.

✉ 79 rue Saint-Dominique, 75007 ☎ 01 47 05 49 75 ⏰ Lunch, dinner
🚇 Invalides

SHOPPING

ANTIQUES
Village Suisse

Very expensive antiques displayed in the former Swiss pavilions
of the 1900 World Exhibition.

✉ 78 avenue de Suffren, 54 rue de la Motte-Picquet, 75015;
www.levillagesuisseparis.com 🚇 La Motte Picquet, Grenelle

BOOKS, CDs, VIDEOS AND HI-FI
Gibert Joseph

Stationery, new and second-hand books, CDs and videos.

✉ 26–30 boulevard Saint-Michel, 75006 ☎ 01 44 41 88 88;
www.gilbertjoseph.com 🚇 Odéon, Cluny-la-Sorbonne

Village Voice

English-language bookshop.

✉ 6 rue Princesse, 75006 ☎ 01 46 33 36 47;
www.villagevoicebookshop.com 🚇 Mabillon

CHILDREN'S SHOPS
Chantelivre

Specialist bookshop dealing with the subjects that interest kids.

✉ 13 rue de Sèvres, 75006 ☎ 01 45 48 87 90 🚇 Sèvres-Babylone

La Maison des Bonbons

Delicious sweets in all shapes.

✉ 14 rue Mouton Duvernet 75014 ☎ 01 45 41 25 55 🚇 Mouton Duvernet

DEPARTMENT STORE
Bon Marché Rive Gauche

The only department store on the Left Bank; famous for its Grande
Epicerie, selling specialities from various countries.

✉ 24 rue de Sèvres, 75007 ☎ 01 44 39 80 00; www.lebonmarche.fr
🚇 Sèvres-Babylone

FASHION
Yohji Yamamoto
Ready-to-wear clothes by the Japanese designer.
✉ 22 rue de Sèvres, 75007 ☎ 01 45 44 29 32 🚇 St-Germain-des-Prés

FOOD AND WINES
Boulangerie Poîlane
See page 80.

La Grande Épicerie de Paris
This huge grocery store is every gourmet's dreamland!
✉ 38 rue de Sèvres, 75007 ☎ 01 44 39 81 00; www.lagrandeepicerie.fr
🚇 Sèvres-Babylone

MISCELLANEOUS GIFTS
Upla
Trendy gift shop.
✉ 5 rue St-Benoît, 75006 ☎ 01 40 15 10 75 🚇 St-Germain des Prés

SHOPPING CENTRES
Marché Saint-Germain
See page 81.

ENTERTAINMENT

CINEMA
La Pagode
La Pagode is wonderfully exotic, with its painted screens and Japanese garden. Shows cult classics and recent arty releases in the original language
✉ 57 bis rue de Babylone, 75007 ☎ 01 45 55 48 48 🚇 St-François Xavier

JAZZ CLUB
Bilboquet
Select establishment at the heart of St-Germain-des-Prés for serious jazz fans.

✉ 13 rue Saint-Benoît, 75006 ☎ 01 45 48 81 84 🚇 St-Germain-des-Prés

THEATRE, DANCE AND OPERA
Odéon, Théâtre de l'Europe
This venue stages classical and contemporary theatre from all over Europe, often in languages other than French.

✉ 2 rue Corneillel, 75006 ☎ 01 44 85 40 00; www.theatre-odeon.fr
🚇 Odéon

Théâtre du Vieux Colombier
The Théâtre du Vieux Colombier offers both classical and contemporary theatre performed by the Comédie-Française troupe.

✉ 21 rue du Vieux Colombier, 75006 ☎ 01 44 39 87 00;
www.comedie-francaise.fr 🚇 St-Sulpice

BARS AND CLUBS
Cubana Café
A little bit of Havana in the heart of Paris – with posters, pictures and slogans, cigars and cocktails.

✉ 45 rue Vavin, 75006 ☎ 01 40 46 80 81; www.cubanacafe.com 🚇 Vavin

Le Petit Journal Montparnasse
A mixture of good food and quality jazz, featuring some of France's finest musicians.

✉ 11 rue du Commandant-Mouchottes, 75014 ☎ 01 43 21 56 70;
www.petitjournal-montparnasse.com 🚇 Montparnasse-Bienvenue

Rhumerie
The colonial atmosphere is the main attraction. Enjoy a cocktail on the terrace.

✉ 166 boulevard St-Germain, 75006 ☎ 01 43 54 28 94;
www.larhumerie.com 🚇 Mabillon

The Louvre to the Arc de Triomphe

The area of western Paris, from the Louvre to the Arc de Triomphe is noted more for its grandeur than its charm. It's full of elegant squares, formal gardens, fashionable shops and luxury hotels.

Without a doubt, the greatest attraction is the Musée du Louvre. Northwest lie the Jardin des Tuileries, place de la Concorde and the Champs-Élysées, which leads to the Arc de Triomphe and on to La Défense. South of the Arc de Triomphe brings you to the Palais de Chaillot, while north of the Louvre are two of Paris's best shopping streets – rue de Rivoli and rue St-Honoré.

ALEXANDRE III, PONT

This is Paris's most ornate bridge, named after the Tsar of Russia to celebrate the Franco-Russian alliance. Its sole arch spanning the Seine is in line with the Invalides on the Left Bank while, on the Right Bank, the avenue Winston Churchill leads straight to the Champs-Elysées. The bridge is decorated with exuberant allegorical sculptures surmounted by gilt horses.

✚ 5B ✉ Cours La Reine/Quai d'Orsay 🚇 Invalides 🚌 63, 83

ARC DE TRIOMPHE

Commissioned by Napoleon, the 50m-high (164ft) Arc de Triomphe was completed by France's last reigning monarch and finally dedicated to the memory of an unknown soldier of the Republic who died during World War I. It stands in line with the Arc de Triomphe du Carrousel near the Louvre and the Grande Arche de la Défense. From the top there is a 360-degree panorama, with, in the foreground, its 12 avenues reaching out like tentacles towards the city beyond.

✚ 2E ✉ Place Charles de Gaulle, 75008 ☎ 01 43 80 31 31 🕐 Oct–Mar daily 10am–10.30pm; Apr–Sep daily 10am–11pm. Closed 1 Jan, 1 May, 25 Dec ✋ Moderate 🍴 Choice of restaurants near by (€–€€€) 🚇 Charles de Gaulle-Etoile 🚌 22, 30, 31, 52, 78, 92 ❓ Video, shops

ART MODERNE DE LA VILLE DE PARIS, MUSÉE D'

The Palais de Tokyo, housing the modern art collections, was built for the 1937 World Exhibition; significantly, one of the main exhibits is a huge work called *La Fée Electricité*, painted by Raoul Dufy for the 'Light Pavilion' at the Exhibition. Most of the major artisitic trends of the 20th century are represented.

✚ 3B ✉ 11 avenue du Président Wilson, 75116 ☎ 01 53 67 40 00 🕐 Tue–Fri 10–5.30, Sat–Sun 10–7. Closed public hols ✋ Inexpensive 🍴 Cafe (€) 🚇 Iéna, Alma-Marceau 🚌 32, 42, 63, 72, 80, 92 ❓ Guided tours (reservations necessary)

ARTS ASIATIQUES-GUIMET, MUSÉE NATIONAL DES/PANTHÉON BOUDDHIQUE

This museum's collections, spanning 5,000 years, illustrate all the major civilizations of the Asian continent, with special emphasis on calligraphy, painting, gold plate and textiles. In addition, carefully restored monumental works from Cambodia and Afghanistan are on display for the first time (➤ 74).

www.museeguimet.fr

🚇 2C ✉ Museum: 6 place d'Iéna; Panthéon Bouddhique: 19 avenue d'Iéna, 75016 ☎ 01 56 52 53 00 🕐 Wed–Mon 10–6 ✋ Moderate 🚇 Boissiére, Iéna 🚌 22, 30, 32, 63, 82

ARTS DÉCORATIFS, MUSÉE DES

The Museum of Decorative Arts is housed in the Marsan wing of the Louvre. The Medieval and Renaissance collections include remarkable altarpieces, religious paintings, 16th-century stained-glass objects of daily life, and fine tapestries (➤ 74).

🚇 9B ✉ 107 rue de Rivoli, 75001 ☎ 01 44 55 57 50 🕐 Tue–Fri 11–6, Sat–Sun 10–6 ✋ Inexpensive 🍴 The main Louvre nearby 🚇 Palais-Royal 🚌 21, 27, 39, 48, 68, 72, 81, 95

BACCARAT, MUSÉE

The prestigious collections of Baccarat crystal housed here illustrate the evolution of styles and manufacturing techniques since 1764: vases, chandeliers, perfume bottles and other objects including candelabra ordered by Tsar Nicholas II of Russia. The most fascinating exhibits are probably the unique pieces specially created by Baccarat for various World Exhibitions since 1855.

🚇 2C ✉ 11 place des Etats-Unis, 75016 ☎ 01 40 22 11 00 🕐 Mon, Wed–Sat 10–6 ✋ Inexpensive 🚇 Iéna, Boissière 🚌 32, 38 48

BALZAC, MAISON DE

Honoré de Balzac lived here from 1840 to 1847. It contains mementoes of his life and work, such as manuscripts, letters, original drawings and prints and a plaster cast that Rodin used as a study for the monumental statue now standing in Montparnasse.

🚇 1A (off map) ✉ 47 rue Raynouard, 75016 ☎ 01 55 74 41 80 🕐 Tue–Sun 10–6. Closed public hols ✋ Free 🚇 Passy, La Muette 🚌 32, 50, 70, 72

CERNUSCHI, MUSÉE

The building houses banker and art collector Henri Cernuschi's
superb collection of ancient Chinese art on the ground floor
(terracottas, bronzes, jades and ceramics) and contemporary
traditional Chinese paintings on the first floor.

➕ 5F ✉ 7 avenue Velasquez, 75008 ☎ 01 45 63 50 75 ⏰ Tue–Sun 10–5.40
✋ Inexpensive 🚇 Villiers 🚌 30, 94

CHAILLOT, PALAIS DE

Designed for the 1937 World Exhibition, the building consists of
two separate pavilions with curved wings, on either side of a vast
terrace decorated with monumental statues. Just below, the
tiered Jardins du Trocadéro extend to the edge of the river. The
ornamental fountain is particularly impressive at night when the
powerful spray of water shines under the spotlights (➤ 74).

The Musée de l'Homme, devoted to Man as a species, contains
items from Africa, Asia and South America, including around 500
musical instruments from around the world.

The Musée de la Marine is devoted to French maritime history
from the 18th century onwards. The extensive collections show
the development of navigational skills and include models of
18th-century sailing ships; they also retrace the history of maritime
transport and great expeditions across the world.

The east wing was seriously damaged by fire in 1997 and the
two museums it contained are now closed. The Musée des
Monuments Français will reopen once building work has finished,
whereas the Musée du Cinéma Henri Langlois will probably move
to new premises in the former American Center in Bercy.
www.mnhn.fr

➕ 1B ✉ Place du Trocadéro, 75016 ☎ Musée de l'Homme: 01 44 05 72 72;
Musée de la Marine: 01 53 65 69 69 ⏰ Musée de l'Homme: Wed–Mon
9.45–5.15, Sat–Sun 10–6.30; closed public hols. Musée de la Marine:
Wed–Mon 10–6; closed 1 Jan, 1 May, 25 Dec ✋ Both museums: moderate
🚇 Trocadéro 🚌 22, 30, 32, 63, 72, 82

CHAMPS-ELYSÉES, LES
See pages 38–39.

CONCORDE, PLACE DE LA
This is undoubtedly the most impressive square in Paris: its stately elegance, its size and its magnificent views are simply breathtaking. Built in the mid-18th century, it was designed by Gabriel who erected two Classical pavilions on either side of the rue Royale; its octagonal shape is emphasized by eight allegorical statues representing major French cities.

The pink granite obelisk from Luxor, offered to the French nation by the viceroy of Egypt in 1836, is at the centre of the square, flanked by two graceful fountains. Two magnificent vistas open up: one towards the Champs-Elysées and Le Louvre beyond the beautiful gates of the Jardin des Tuileries; the other towards the Madeleine at the end of the rue Royale and the Assemblée Nationale across the pont de la Concorde.

✚ 7C ✉ 75008 🚇 Concorde 🚌 42, 73, 84, 94

FAUBOURG ST-HONORÉ

This 'suburb' is centred on the very long street of the same name, running parallel to the Champs-Elysées and famous for its haute couture establishments and luxury boutiques as well as for the Palais de l'Elysée, the official residence of the French president.

Leading fashion houses have been established in the area for over a hundred years: Louis Féraud, Christian Lacroix and Lanvin are still in the rue du Faubourg St-Honoré, but the majority are now in the avenue Montaigne across the Champs-Elysées. Opposite the British Embassy, No 54 opens into a couple of courtyards surrounded by boutiques selling beautiful furniture, objets d'art and paintings. Many modern art galleries line the perpendicular avenue Matignon, while the avenue Gabriel, which runs along the Champs-Elysées gardens past the American Embassy, makes a peaceful stroll through this select area.

🔆 5D 🖂 75008 🚇 St-Philippe-du-Roule, Madeleine
🚌 52 ❓ A stamp market takes place near the Rond-Point des Champs-Elysées on Thu, Sat and Sun 9–7

GALLIÉRA, MUSÉE

This museum of fashion is housed in a neo-Renaissance mansion dating from the late 19th century, the Palais Galliéra. Its rich collections of urban fashion, are shown in temporary exhibitions from the 18th century to the present and are continually being extended with donations from prestigious fashion houses (Dior, Yves St-Laurent) and well-known personalities. In addition to the costumes (several thousand in all), there are etchings and photographs connected with fashion.

🔆 2C 🖂 Palais Galliéra, 10 avenue Pierre Ier de Serbie, 75016 ☎ 01 56 52 86 20 🕐 Tue–Sun 10–6 ✋ Moderate 🚇 Iéna 🚌 32, 42, 63, 72, 80, 82, 92 ❓ Children's workshops

GRAND PALAIS

Built at the same time as the Pont Alexandre III for the 1900 World
Exhibition, this enormous steel-and-glass structure, concealed
behind stone walls, is typical of the *belle époque* style: Ionic
columns line the imposing façade and colossal bronze statues
decorate the four corners (➤ 74). Major international art
exhibitions – Tutankhamun, Renoir, Gauguin and Picasso, to name
but a few – are traditionally held in the Galeries Nationales, on
the Champs-Elysées side of the building.

The west part of the Grand Palais houses the Palais de la
Découverte, inaugurated in 1937 to bring science within the
grasp of the general public and keep them informed of the latest
scientific developments. There are interactive experiments,
documentary films and a planetarium.

✚ 5C ✉ Galeries Nationales: avenue du Général Eisenhower, 75008;
Palais de la Découverte, avenue Franklin-D-Roosevelt, 75008 ☎ Galeries
Nationales: 01 44 13 17 30; Palais Découverte: 01 56 43 20 21 🕐 Galeries
Nationales: variable; Palais Découverte: Tue–Sat 9.30–6, Sun 10–7
💰 Galeries Nationales: variable; Palais Découverte: moderate
🍴 Café-bar (€) 🚇 Champs-Elysées-Clemenceau 🚌 28, 32, 42, 72, 73,
80, 83, 93

LA GRANDE ARCHE DE LA DÉFENSE

See pages 40–41.

JACQUEMART-ANDRÉ, MUSÉE

This elegant 19th-century mansion houses the remarkable collections of European art bequeathed by the wealthy widow of a banker to the Institut de France. French 18th-century art includes paintings by Boucher, Chardin, Greuze and Watteau, as well as sculptures by Houdon and Pigalle, furniture, Beauvais tapestries and objets d'art. There are also 17th-century Dutch and Flemish masterpieces and Italian Renaissance art including works by Mantegna, Donatello, Botticelli and Uccello.

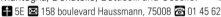

✚ 5E ✉ 158 boulevard Haussmann, 75008 ☎ 01 45 62 11 59 🕐 Daily 10–6 ✋ Moderate 🍴 Tea room (€) Ⓜ Miromesnil, St-Philippe-du-Roule 🚌 22, 28, 43, 52, 54, 80, 83, 84, 93

JEU DE PAUME

One of two pavilions built in the late 19th century at the entrance of the Jardin des Tuileries, the Jeu de Paume was intended for the practice of a game similar to tennis. It later housed the national collection of Impressionist paintings until it was transferred to the Musée d'Orsay. Now it is now exclusively devoted to the art of photography, holding thematic and monographic exhibitions from the 19th century to the 21st century.

✚ 7C ✉ 1 place de la Concorde, 75001 ☎ 01 47 03 12 52 🕐 Wed–Fri 12–7, Sat–Sun 10–7, Tue 12–9.30 ✋ Moderate 🍴 Café (€) Ⓜ Concorde 🚌 24, 42, 52, 72, 73, 84, 94 ❓ Shop

LE LOUVRE

See pages 44–45.

MADELEINE, ÉGLISE DE LA

Work started on this imposing neoclassical building in 1764, and the church was eventually consecrated in 1845 (➤ 76). It is an impressive Graeco-Roman temple completely surrounded by tall Corinthian columns. Steps lead up to the entrance, which is surmounted by a monumental pediment. The interior is decorated with sculptures by Rude and Pradier; the magnificent organ was made by Cavaillé-Coll in 1846.

➕ 7D ✉ Place de la Madeleine, 75008 ☎ 01 44 51 69 00 🕐 Mon–Sat 7–7, Sun 8–1.30, 3.30–7; public hols variable ✋ Free 🚇 Madeleine 🚌 24, 42, 52, 84, 94 ❓ Shops

MARMOTTAN-MONET, MUSÉE

The museum was named after Paul Marmottan, who bequeathed his house and his private collections of Renaissance and 18th- and 19th-century art to the Institut de France. These were later enriched by several bequests, including 100 paintings by Monet donated by his son: detailed studies of Monet's garden in Giverny,

particularly a group of *nymphéas* (water lilies) paintings, provide insights into the artist's approach, and there are paintings of Rouen Cathedral (executed in different light conditions according to the time of day) and of the River Thames in London. Most important of all, perhaps, is a relatively early work, called *Impression, Soleil levant* (1872), which created a sensation at the time and gave its name to the Impressionist movement (▶ 75). There are also interesting works by Monet's contemporaries, Renoir, Pissarro, Sisley, Morisot and Gauguin.

➕ 1B (off map) ✉ 2 rue Louis Boilly, 75016 ☎ 01 42 24 07 02 🕐 Tue–Sun 10–6. Closed 1 Jan, 1 May, 25 Dec ✋ Moderate 🍴 Cafés and restaurants (€–€€) in nearby place de la Muette 🚇 La Muette 🚌 22, 32, 52, 63 ❓ Shops

NISSIM DE CAMONDO, MUSÉE

This museum offers a delightful journey back into the 18th century. The interior is arranged as an authentic 18th-century private home, including wall panelling, Aubusson and Savonnerie tapestries, paintings by Vigée-Lebrun and Hubert Robert, sculptures by Houdon and Sèvres and Chantilly porcelain.

🚻 5F ✉ 63 rue de Monceau, 75008 ☎ 01 53 89 06 50 🕒 Wed–Sun 10–5. Closed 1 Jan, 14 Jul, 25 Dec 🖐 Inexpensive 🚇 Villiers 🚌 84, 94 ❓ Guided tours

OPÉRA GARNIER

The Palais Garnier (named after its architect) was built in 1875 in neoclassical style, but the decoration is unmistakably late 19th century and includes a group of statues called *La Danse* by Carpeaux, a copy of the original now in the Musée d'Orsay. Inside, the grand staircase and the foyer are magnificent. In the main hall, restored to its original splendour, visitors can now fully appreciate the ceiling decorated by Chagall.

The museum contains paintings, watercolours and pastels illustrating the history of opera and ballet from the 18th century to the present day, mainly through portraits of famous singers, dancers and composers.

🚻 9D ✉ Place de l'Opéra, 75009 ☎ 01 41 10 08 10 🕒 Daily 10–4.30. Closed 1 Jan, 1 May and matinee performances 🖐 Moderate 🚇 Opéra 🚌 20, 21, 22, 27, 29, 42, 52, 53, 56, 81, 95 ❓ Guided tours at 12.30, shops

ORANGERIE, MUSÉE NATIONAL DE L'

The Orangerie houses the Walter-Guillaume Collection, consisting mainly of Impressionist and 20th-century paintings, and a set of monumental paintings by Monet, representing the famous *nymphéas* (water lilies) in the artist's garden at Giverny.

✚ 7B ✉ Place de la Concorde, Jardin des Tuileries, 75001 ☎ 01 42 97 48 16 🕐 Closed for restructuring 🚇 Concorde 🚌 24, 42, 52, 72, 73, 84, 94 ❓ Guided tours, shops

PALAIS-ROYAL

The palace built by Richelieu and bequeathed to the king on the cardinal's death now houses the Ministry of Culture and two important constitutional bodies, but the gardens are accessible through archways situated all round. Enclosed by arcading on three sides and an elegant double colonnade along the fourth,

they are a haven of peace. An 18th-century addition to the original building houses the Comédie-Française, France's national theatre. From the place André Malraux in front, the Opéra Garnier can be seen at the top of the avenue de l'Opéra.

To the east of the Palais-Royal, off the rue Croix des Petits Champs, the Galerie Véro-Dodat is one of several elegant arcades in the area.

✚ 9B ✉ Place du Palais-Royal, 75001 🕐 Jardin: daily 8am–11pm (midnight in summer) 🖐 Jardin: free access 🍽 In the gardens (€€) 🚇 Palais-Royal

PARFUM, MUSÉE DU

The history of perfume from the time of the ancient Egyptians to the present is the fascinating subject of this museum, housed within the Fragonard perfumery, in two different places, both near the opera house.

www.fragonard.com

✚ 8D ✉ 9 rue Scribe, 75009; 39 boulevard des Capucines, 75002 🖐 Free

127

TUILERIES, JARDIN DES

This formal French-style garden was laid out by Le Nôtre in the 17th century. It deteriorated over the years through extensive use and the increasing effects of pollution, but has been renovated. The stately central alleyway stretches in a straight line from the flower beds near the Arc de Triomphe du Carrousel to the place de la Concorde, where an octagonal ornamental pool is surrounded by various statues and flanked by terraces. On either side of the alleyway are groups of allegorical statues. There is a lovely view of the river and the gardens with the Louvre in the background from the Terrasse du Bord de l'Eau running along the riverbank.

✚ 8B ✉ Rue de Rivoli, 75001 🕓 Apr–Sep daily 7.30am–8pm; Oct–Mar daily 7.30am–7pm 🖐 Free 🍴 Cafeterias (€) 🚇 Tuileries (access from rue de Rivoli); Palais-Royal (access from the Louvre) 🚌 24, 68, 72, 73, 84, 94

VENDÔME, PLACE

This square illustrates Louis XIV's style at its best, Classical and elegant without being too emphatic. It was designed by Jules Hardouin-Mansart at the end of the 17th century and an equestrian statue of the King was placed in its centre. However, the statue was destroyed during the Revolution and in 1810 Napoleon had a tall bronze-clad column erected in its place, somewhat spoiling the architectural harmony. Today Paris's top jewellers are based here.

✚ 8C ✉ 75001 🚇 Opéra 🚌 72

HOTELS

George V (€€€)
See page 78.

Hotel Astrid (€€)
No two bedrooms are the same in the Astrid, which lies close to the Champs-Élysées. Styles include country (pine furniture) and romantic (brass bedframes and chandeliers).
✉ 27 avenue Carnot, 75017 ☎ 01 44 09 26 00; www.hotel-astrid.com
🚇 Charles de Gaulle-Étoile

Hôtel Galileo (€€)
Modern refined hotel near the Champs-Elysées with air-conditioning and well-appointed bedrooms; a few have verandas.
✉ 54 rue Galilée, 75008 ☎ 01 47 20 66 06 🚇 George V

Hôtel Franklin-Roosevelt (€€€)
See page 78.

Hotel du Louvre (€€–€€€)
This historic hotel faces the Opéra Garnier and the Louvre Museum. Its 200 guestrooms and suites are decorated in a variety of styles
✉ Place André Malraux, 75001 ☎ 01 44 58 38 38; www.concorde-hotels.com 🚇 Palais Royal-Musée du Louvre

Hôtel Meurice (€€€)
See page 79.

Hôtel Relais du Louvre (€€)
Warm colours, antique furniture and modern comfort, a stone's throw from the Louvre.
✉ 19 rue des Prêtres Saint-Germain-l'Auxerrois, 75001 ☎ 01 40 41 96 42; www.relaisdulouvre.com 🚇 Louvre-Rivoli

Hôtel Ritz Paris (€€€)
See page 79.

Millennium Hôtel Paris-Opéra (€€–€€€)
The rooms in this stylish art deco hotel, in the heart of the
business area, have period furnishings and sparkling white
bathrooms.
✉ 12 boulevard Haussmann, 75009 ☎ 01 49 49 16 00; www.millennium-
hotels.co 🚇 Richelieu-Drouot

RESTAURANTS

L'Alsace (€€)
Alsatian specialities and seafood; terrace in summer.
✉ 39 avenue des Champs-Elysées, 75008 ☎ 01 53 93 97 00 🕐 24 hours
🚇 Franklin-D Roosevelt

Bon (€€)
Trendy restaurant; some vegetarian dishes.
✉ 25 rue de la Pompe, 75016 ☎ 01 40 72 70 00 🕐 Lunch, dinner
🚇 La Muette

La Butte Chaillot (€€)
Refined cuisine served in a striking contemporary setting.
✉ 110 bis avenue Kléber, 75016 ☎ 01 47 27 88 88 🕐 Lunch, dinner; closed
Sat lunch and 3 weeks in Aug 🚇 Trocadéro, Boissière

Chez Clément Élysées (€)
Home style cooking.
✉ 123 avenue des Champs-Élysées, 75008 ☎ 01 40 73 87 00 🕐 Lunch,
dinner 🚇 Charles de Gaulle-Étoile

Grand Véfour (€€€)
See page 63.

Le Jardin (€€€)
Mediterranean-style haute cuisine; a speciality is the lobster
roasted with spices.

✉ Hôtel Royal Monceau, 37 avenue Hoche, 75008 ☎ 01 42 99 98 70
🕐 Lunch, dinner; closed Sat, Sun, public hols 🚇 Charles de Gaulle-Etoile

Jipangue (€–€€)
Excellent Japanese cuisine.
✉ 96 rue La Boétie, 75008 ☎ 01 45 63 77 00 🕐 Lunch, dinner; closed Sat
lunch and Sun 🚇 St-Philipe-du-Roule

Lucas Carton (€€€)
See page 63.

Le Piano des Saisons (€)
Attractive new restaurant; seafood cuisine from southwest
France.
✉ 11 rue Treilhard, 75008 ☎ 01 45 61 09 46 🕐 Lunch, dinner; closed
Sat–Sun 🚇 Miromesnil, St-Augustin

Stresa (€€)
Trendy Italian restaurant; booking advisable.
✉ 7 rue de Chambiges, 75008 ☎ 01 47 23 51 62 🕐 Lunch, dinner; closed
Sat dinner, Sun lunch, Aug and Christmas 🚇 Alma-Marceau

Timgad (€€€)
See page 63.

SHOPPING

ANTIQUES
Louvre des Antiquaires
See page 81.

BOOKS, CDs, VIDEOS AND HI-FI
FNAC
See page 80.

DEPARTMENT STORES
Galeries Lafayette
See page 81.

Monoprix

Chain of department stores for the budget-conscious. There is a
large branch at the back of Au Printemps.

✉ 52 avenue des Champs-Elysées, 75008 ☎ 01 53 77 65 65
Ⓜ Franklin-D Roosevelt

Au Printemps

See page 80.

FASHION – BOUTIQUES AND ACCESSORIES
Hermès

Silk scarves, leather goods.

✉ 24 rue du Faubourg Saint-Honoré, 75008 ☎ 01 40 17 47 17 Ⓜ Concorde

Madelios

Male fashion from city suits to casuals and accessories.

✉ 23 boulevard de la Madeleine, 75001 ☎ 01 53 45 00 00 Ⓜ Madeleine

Walter Steiger

Luxury shoes for men and women.

✉ 83 rue du Faubourg Saint-Honoré, 75008 ☎ 01 42 66 65 08
Ⓜ Miromesnil

FOOD AND WINES
Dubois et Fils

This temple to an amazing range of cheese supplies Paris's top
restaurants.

✉ 80 rue de Tocqueville, 75017 ☎ 01 42 27 11 38 Ⓜ Malesherbes, Villiers

Les Caves Augé

For wine lovers. This is the oldest wine shop in Paris.

✉ 116 boulevard Haussmann, 75008 ☎ 01 45 22 16 97 🕓 Closed one week
in Aug Ⓜ École-Militaire

Fauchon and Hédiard

See page 80.

Lenôtre
Succulent cakes that melt in the mouth!
✉ 15 boulevard de Courcelles, 75008 ☎ 01 45 63 87 63 Ⓜ Villiers

MISCELLANEOUS GIFTS
Bernardaud
Porcelain, tableware, jewellery, original gifts.
✉ 11 rue Royale, 75008 ☎ 01 47 42 82 66 Ⓜ Concorde, Madeleine

Maison du Chocolat
Want to try the best chocolate in Paris?
✉ 225 rue du Faubourg Saint-Honoré, 75008 ☎ 01 42 27 39 44 Ⓜ Ternes

SHOPPING CENTRES
Carrousel du Louvre
See page 80.

Drugstore Publicis
Unexpectedly situated at the top of the Champs-Elysées, just a
stone's throw from the Arc de Triomphe, this shopping mall has
a restaurant and a selection of gift/souvenir shops.
✉ 133 avenue des Champs-Elysées, 75008 ☎ 01 44 43 79 00 Ⓜ Charles de
Gaulle-Etoile

TOY SHOP
La Boutique de Floriane
Le Nain Bleu
The most famous toy shop in Paris.
✉ 408 rue Saint-Honoré, 75008 ☎ 01 42 60 39 01 Ⓜ Concorde, Madeleine

ENTERTAINMENT
CABARET AND MUSIC HALL
Crazy Horse Saloon
One of the best shows in Paris with beautiful girls and striking
colours and lights.
✉ 12 avenue George V, 75008 ☎ 01 47 23 32 32 Ⓜ Alma-Marceau

Le Lido
See page 72.

Olympia
The most popular music-hall in France has been completely refurbished.
✉ 28 boulevard des Capucines, 75009 ☎ 08 92 68 33 68;
www.olympiahall.com 🚇 Opéra

CONCERT VENUES
Salle Pleyel
Traditional concert hall, named after one of France's most famous piano-makers, recently refurbished, and home to the Orchestre de Paris.
✉ 252 rue du Faubourg Saint-Honoré, 75008 ☎ 01 45 61 53 00 🚇 Ternes, Charles de Gaulle-Etoile

Theâtre des Champs-Elysées
See page 73.

SPORT
Hippodrome d'Auteuil
Steeplechasing; Grand Steeplechase de Paris, mid-June.
✉ Bois de Boulogne, 75016 ☎ 01 40 71 47 47 🚇 Porte d'Auteuil

Hippodrome de Longchamp
Flat-racing; Grand Prix de Paris in late June, Prix de l'Arc de Triomphe in October.
✉ Bois de Boulogne, 75016 ☎ 01 44 30 75 00 🚇 Porte Maillot and 🚌 244

Parc des Princes
See page 73.

Roland Garros
Venue every year in late May and early June for the tennis tournament.
✉ 2 avenue Gordon Bennett, 75016 ☎ 01 47 43 48 00 🚇 Porte d'Auteuil

Le Marais and Bastille

Le Marais was once an area of marshland on the Right Bank of the Seine. In the 13th century, the area was drained and cultivated by monks and the Knights Templar. However, it was the construction of the place des Vosges at the beginning of the 17th century and the subsequent rapid urbanization of the district that produced a wealth of beautiful domestic architecture and gave Le Marais its unique character. When fashions changed in the late 18th century, the district gradually became derelict and had to wait until the 1970s to be rediscovered and renovated.

To the west is the Beaubourg district, renowned for its ultra-modern Les Halles shopping centre, and the Centre Georges Pompidou, with its world-famous art collections. To the east lies the Bastille district, forever associated with the French Revolution when the dreaded fortress was stormed by the people of Paris on 14 July, 1789, and later razed to the ground. Today the area is a lively nightspot with a great selection of bars and restaurants. Further east, on the edge of the city, is Cimetière du Père-Lachaise, Paris's most famous cemetery.

ARTS ET MÉTIERS-TECHNIQUES, MUSÉE DES

This quirky museum is devoted to the artistic aspect of scientific and technical achievements.

✚ 12C ✉ 60 rue Réaumur, 75003 ☎ 01 53 01 82 00 🕓 Tue–Sun 10–6 (Thu to 9.30pm) ✋ Moderate 🚇 Arts et Métiers

BASTILLE

The outline of the Bastille can be seen on the paving stones covering the entire place de la Bastille. In the centre stands a 50m-high (164ft) column erected in memory of the victims of the 1830 and 1848 Revolutions, who were buried beneath the base and whose names are carved on the shaft. The column is surmounted by the gilt winged figure of the Spirit of Liberty by Dumont.

The **Opéra Bastille** was inaugurated for the bicentenary of the 1789 Revolution. Designed by the Canadian architect Carlos Ott, the Opéra National de Paris-Bastille is a harmonious building with a curved façade in several shades of grey that glitters in the sun and gently glows at night. The acoustics of the main auditorium, which can accommodate 2,700 spectators, are superb and the stage is one of the most sophisticated in the world.

Just south of the opera house, a disused railway viaduct has been converted into workshops and showrooms known as the **Viaduc des Arts** illustrating a number of traditional crafts; the Ateliers du Cuivre et de l'Argent (copper and silver workshops) are particularly interesting and there is a small museum.

✚ 24L

Opéra Bastille

✉ Place de la Bastille, 75012 ☎ Recorded information: 01 40 01 19 70 🕓 Listen to the recorded information. Closed Sun ✋ Moderate 🍴 Bar 🚇 Bastille 🚌 20, 29, 65, 69, 76, 86, 87, 91 ❓ Guided tours, shops

Viaduc des Arts

✉ 9–129 avenue Daumesnil, 75012 🕓 Variable; most workshops open Sun 🍴 Nearby (€) 🚇 Bastille, Ledru-Rollin, Reuilly-Diderot

BIBLIOTHÈQUE NATIONALE DE FRANCE

Until 1996, the BN, as Parisians call it, was housed in Cardinal Mazarin's former palace situated at the back of the Palais-Royal, extended many times and now stretching from the rue de Richelieu to the rue Vivienne. However, with around 13 million books and as many prints and photographs, it had long been overcrowded. The building of a new library along the river in the 13th *arrondissement* was President Mitterrand's last 'Grand Projet'. The BNF, as it is now called, occupies two sites known as 'Richelieu' and 'François Mitterrand'.

The new library houses the huge stock of printed books and documents and is intended to serve as a public library and a research centre equipped with the most modern means of data transmission. Four corner towers looking like open books surround an imposing base with a central garden where the reading rooms are situated.

The Richelieu building houses manuscripts, prints and medals and holds exhibitions in the Galerie Mansart (Galerie de Photographie), the Galerie Mazarine (which has a magnificent painted ceiling) and the Crypte. The Cabinet des Médailles et des Antiques displays coins and medals from antiquity to the present day as well as objets d'art, cameos and bronzes from the former royal collections.

Two attractive arcades linked to the library, the Galerie Vivienne and the Galerie Colbert, offer an unexpected insight into Parisian social life in the 19th century. **www.bnf.fr**

✚ 10C ✉ Richelieu: 58 rue de Richelieu, 75002; François Mitterrand: quai François Mauriac, 75013 ☎ Richelieu: 01 53 79 59 59; guided tours: 01 53 79 86 87; François Mitterrand: 01 53 79 59 59 🕐 Richelieu: Galeries and Crypt: Tue–Sat 10–7, Sun 12–7. Cabinet des Médailles: Mon–Sat 1–5, Sun 12–6. François Mitterrand: visits of the building on Tue–Sat 2, Sun 3 by appointment only ✋ Richelieu: moderate; François Mitterrand: free 🍴 Richelieu: restaurant in Galerie Vivienne (€) 🚇 Richelieu: Bourse, Palais-Royal-Musée du Louvre; François Mitterrand: Quai de la Gare 🚌 Richelieu: 29, 39, 48; François Mitterrand: 62, 89

CARNAVALET, MUSÉE

The Hôtel Carnavalet was the residence of diarist, Madame de Sévigné, who depicted Parisian society at the time of Louis XIV with a great deal of humour. Note the 16th-century lions guarding the entrance and Louis XIV's statue by Coysevox in the centre of the courtyard. In 1989, the museum (▶ 74) was linked to the nearby Hôtel Le Peletier de St Fargeau, which dates from the late 17th century. The Hôtel Carnavalet deals with the period from the origins of the city to 1789, with mementoes of Madame de Sévigné and splendid Louis XV and Louis XVI furniture. The Hôtel Le Peletier de St Fargeau houses collections from 1789 to the present day. The Revolution is extensively illustrated, while the 19th and 20th centuries are represented by a number of reconstructions such as Marcel Proust's bedroom and the art nouveau reception room of the Café de Paris.

✚ 23L ✉ 23 rue de Sévigné, 75003 ☎ 01 44 59 58 58 🕐 Tue–Sun 10–5.40. Closed some public hols
✋ Free, except for some temporary exhibitions
🍴 Restaurants and cafés nearby in rue des Francs-Bourgeois (€–€€€) 🚇 Saint-Paul 🚌 29, 69, 76, 96
❓ Guided tours, shops

CENTRE GEORGES POMPIDOU
See pages 36–37.

COGNACQ-JAY, MUSÉE
The collections of 18th-century European art bequeathed to the city of Paris by Ernest Cognacq and his wife Louise Jay, founders of the Samaritaine department stores, are displayed in one of the beautiful mansions of Le Marais. The refinement of the Enlightenment period is illustrated by the works of French artists Watteau, Chardin, Fragonard and La Tour, and also by Tiepolo, Guardi and Reynolds. The Rembrandt adds a welcome contrasting note. Various objets d'art, including Saxe and Sèvres porcelain, are exhibited in glass cabinets.

✚ 23M ✉ Hôtel Donon, 8 rue Elzévir, 75003 ☎ 01 40 27 07 21 🕐 Tue–Sun 10–5.40. Closed public hols
✋ Free 🍴 Near by (€–€€) 🚇 Saint-Paul 🚌 29
❓ Guided tours, bookshop

GRANDS BOULEVARDS

These busy arteries, stretching from the place de la République to the Madeleine and lined with cinemas, theatres, cafés and shops, have today fallen victim to their success, choked by traffic jams and disfigured by aggressive neon signs, cheap snack bars and general neglect. The 'boulevards' were laid out as a tree-lined promenade in the 17th century, when some of the city's medieval fortifications were demolished; two ceremonial arches, the Porte St-Martin and the Porte St-Denis, replaced the town gates.

The popularity of the boulevards peaked during the 19th century, with popular attractions in the east (theatre, dancing, circus and busking) and more refined entertainment in the west, especially after the building of the opera house. Several shopping arcades were also opened, including the Passage des Panoramas in boulevard Montmartre, and at the end of the century, one of the first cinemas was inaugurated in boulevard St-Denis by the Lumière brothers.

Today, the boulevards still attract crowds of cinema- and theatregoers but their shabby appearance also encourages a rowdy element, particularly between the Porte St-Martin and the rue de Richelieu. Fortunately, complete renovation is under way.

✚ 9D ✉ From east to west: boulevards St-Martin, St-Denis, de Bonne Nouvelle, Poissonnière, Montmartre, des Italiens, des Capucines and de la Madeleine 🚇 République, Strasbourg-St-Denis, Bonne Nouvelle, Rue Montmartre, Richelieu-Drouot, Opéra, Madeleine

LES HALLES

Paris's legendary food market has long gone from the centre of the capital, but the name is here to stay, tinged for many Parisians with a certain nostalgia, for when the 19th-century steel-and-glass 'pavillons de Baltard' were removed in 1969 and the noisy activity of the market suddenly stopped, the character of this popular district changed beyond recognition. A vast gaping hole was left between one of the most beautiful churches in Paris and a lovely

Renaissance fountain. A commercial and cultural complex was built underground with a central patio surrounded by glass-roofed galleries that barely reach ground level. Above ground, a garden was laid over the remaining space, with a children's area and shaded walks and more graceful steel-and-glass structures. The underground complex comprises shops, restaurants, a swimming pool, an auditorium, a gymnasium and a tropical greenhouse.

A huge stone head leaning against a hand decorates the semicircular paved area in front of the Église St-Eustache. The latter was built over a period of a hundred years, in a blend of late Gothic, Renaissance and neoclassical styles. From the church, a path leads across the gardens to the square des Innocents and the beautiful Renaissance fountain, built and carved in the mid-16th century by Pierre Lescot and Jean Goujon, who also worked on the Louvre.

✚ 11B ✉ Rue Pierre Lescot, rue Rambuteau, rue Berger, 75001
🍴 In the complex (€) 🚇 Les Halles 🚌 29, 38, 47

HÔTEL DE VILLE

The town hall of the city of Paris has been standing on this site since the 14th century. Destroyed by fire during the Paris Commune in 1871, it was rebuilt almost straight away in neo-Renaissance style. On the exterior are 136 statues representing famous historic figures. Nearby stands the 52m-high (170ft) Tour St-Jacques, the only remaining part of a demolished church. In 1648, Pascal used the tower to verify his experiments on the weight of air. Later, a meteorological station was set up at the top and the tower became the property of the city of Paris.

On the east side of the town hall, the Église St-Gervais-St-Protais is a splendid example of a successful blend of Flamboyant Gothic and Classical styles.

🕂 21L ✉ Place de l'Hôtel de Ville, 75004 ☎ 01 42 76 5- 49 🕒 Guided tour by appointment only 🖐 Free 🚇 Hôtel de Ville 🚌 38, 47, 58, 67, 70, 72, 74, 75, 96

LE MARAIS

Le Marais, which extends from the Hôtel de Ville to the place de la

Bastille, offers visitors narrow picturesque streets, cafés and bistros, elegant mansions, tiny boutiques and a lively population that includes an important Jewish community. It is also one of the favourite haunts of the gay community.

Around every corner is another delightful mansion. These houses are no longer privately owned: some have been turned into museums, sometimes with striking results (Musée Picasso, ➤ 145). One of the most imposing, the Hôtel de Soubise, houses the **Musée de l'Histoire de France**, where historic documents are displayed amidst a profusion of Louis XV decoration. An unusual museum dedicated to hunting and nature (**Musée de la Chasse et de la Nature**) is housed in the Hôtel de Guénégaud des Brosses, built by François Mansart (currently closed for restructuring). Here hunting arms dating from prehistory until the 19th century are on display, plus paintings and decorative arts on the subject of hunting.

Musée de l'Histoire de France

🕂 22M ✉ Hôtel de Soubise, 60 rue des Francs-Bourgeois, 75003 ☎ 01 40 27 60 96 🕒 Wed–Mon 1.45–5.45 🖐 Inexpensive 🚇 Hôtel de Ville 🚌 29, 75, 96 ❓ Shop

Musée de la Chasse et de la Nature

🕂 22M ✉ Hôtel de Guénégaud des Brosses, 60 rue des Archives, 75003 ☎ 01 53 01 92 40 🕒 Currently undergoing renovation 🖐 Moderate 🚇 Hôtel de Ville 🚌 29, 75

PAVILLON DE L'ARSENAL

The late 19th-century iron-and-glass building houses an information centre devoted to Paris's urban planning and architecture throughout its troubled history. The permanent exhibition 'Paris, visite guidée' (Paris, a city in the making) shows the constant evolution of the cityscape by means of a dynamic, chronological display covering the ground, walls and ceiling of the main hall, with models, films and interactive terminals.

www.pavillon-arsenal.com

✚ 23K ✉ 21 boulevard Morland, 75004 ☎ 01 42 76 33 97 🕐 Tue–Sat 10.30–6.30, Sun 11–7 ✋ Free 🚇 Sully-Morland 🚌 67, 86, 87

PÈRE-LACHAISE, CIMETIÈRE DU

The rising ground and abundant vegetation give this cemetery a romantic atmosphere in spite of the great number of unsightly funeral monuments. Many famous people are buried here, including Chopin, Molière, Oscar Wilde, Delacroix, Balzac, even the unhappy lovers Héloïse and Abélard. One of the most visited graves is that of Jim Morrison, lead singer of The Doors. In the southeast corner stands the Mur des Fédérés where the last 'communards' were shot in 1871.

✚ 12C (off map) ✉ Boulevard de Ménilmontant, 75020 ☎ 01 55 25 82 10
🕐 Mon–Fri 8–6, Sat 8.30–6, Sun 9–6 (5.30 in winter) ✋ Free
🚇 Père-Lachaise ❓ Guided tours (in English) Sat 3 in summer

PICASSO, MUSÉE

The Picasso collection was brought together after the artist's

death and consists of works donated to the State by his family in lieu of death duties, and his private collection – together totalling more than 200 paintings, sculptures, prints, drawings and ceramics. The Hôtel Salé, at the heart of the historic Marais, was chosen to house this important collection. Like many other mansions in the area, it had been neglected and underwent extensive renovation to turn it into a museum. The interior decoration is very discreet, focusing attention on the beautiful stone staircase with its elegant wrought-iron banister.

Displayed in chronological order, the works illustrate the different phases of Picasso's artistic creation and the various techniques he used, from the blue period tainted with a certain pessimism

(*Autoportrait bleu*), through the more optimistic pink period, to the successive Cubist periods. The tour of the museum is a fascinating journey in the company of one of the most forceful creative minds of this century. Picasso's private collection includes works by Renoir, Cézanne, Rousseau, Braque and others.
www.musee-picasso.fr
✚ 23M ✉ Hôtel Salé, 5 rue de Thorigny, 75003 ☎ 01 42 71 25 21
🕐 Apr–Sep Wed–Mon 9.30–6; Oct–Mar Wed–Mon 5.30. Closed 1 Jan, 25 Dec ✋ Moderate 🚇 St-Paul, Saint-Sébastien Froissart, Chemin Vert
🚌 29, 69, 75, 96 ❓ Guided tours, shop

VOSGES, PLACE DES

This is Paris's oldest square and perhaps the loveliest for its moderate size, its discreet charm, its delightful brick-and-stone architecture and its peaceful central garden. We owe this brilliant piece of town planning to 'Good King Henri' (Henri IV) whose initiative launched the development of Le Marais. The square is lined with identical pavilions over continuous arcading, dormer windows breaking up the monotony of the dark slate roofs; in the centre of the south and north sides stand two higher pavilions, known respectively as the Pavillon du Roi and

Pavillon de la Reine. The square changed names during the Revolution and was finally called 'place des Vosges' in 1800 in honour of the first *département* to pay its taxes!

Number 6, where Victor Hugo (1805–85) lived for 16 years, is now a museum (**Maison de Victor Hugo**), containing family mementoes, furniture, portraits, drawings by the writer himself as well as reconstructions of the various homes Hugo lived in.

✚ 23L ✉ 75004 🚇 St-Paul, Bastille, Chemin Vert 🚌 20, 65, 69, 76

Maison de Victor Hugo

✉ 6 place des Vosges, 75004 ☎ 01 42 72 10 16 🕐 Tue–Sun 10–5.40.
Closed public hols 🖐 Free 🍴 Restaurants nearby 🚇 Bastille 🚌 69, 76
↔ Musée Carnavalet, place de la Bastille

HOTELS

Corail Hôtel (€)
The Corail, located close to the Gare de Lyon métro, RER and train station, is popular with businesspeople. Rooms may lack character but are comfortable.

✉ 23 rue de Lyon, 75012 ☎ 43 43 23 54; www.hotel-paris-corail.com
🚇 Gare de Lyon

Hôtel Agora (€)
The Agora is close to Les Halles and the Centre Pompidou. It has a delightful interior that blends ancient and modern; bedrooms on the top floor are the most pleasant. Most rooms have shower/WC only, but some have baths for an extra charge.

✉ 7 rue de la Cossonnerie, 75001 ☎ 01 42 33 46 02 🚇 Les Halles

Hôtel Beaumarchais (€)
All the rooms in this reasonably priced hotel have bathrooms, with walls and fabrics in fun, primary colours or soothing ochres.The Beaumarchais is gay-friendly but not exclusively gay.

✉ 3 rue Oberkampf, 75011 ☎ 01 53 36 86 86; www.hotelbeaumarchais.com
🚇 Oberkampf

Hôtel Caron de Beaumarchais (€€)
Recently restored 18th-century town house in the Marais; refined period decoration and air-conditioning in all rooms.

✉ 12 rue Vieille-du-Temple, 75004 ☎ 01 42 72 34 12;
www.carondebeaumarchais.com 🚇 Hôtel de Ville, Saint-Paul-le-Marais

Hôtel Claude Bernard (€€–€€€)
See page 78.

Hôtel Place des Vosges (€)
See page 79.

Hotel St-Paul Le Marais (€€)

The St-Paul occupies a former 17th-century convent, close to the Musée Carnavalet. Breakfast is served in a stone-vaulted room.
✉ 8 rue de Sévigné, 75004 ☎ 01 48 04 97 27; www.hotel-paris-marais.com
🚇 St-Paul

RESTAURANTS

Les Amognes (€€)

Bistro serving imaginative cuisine in a relaxed atmosphere.
✉ 243 rue du Faubourg St-Antoine, 75011 ☎ 01 43 72 73 05 🕐 Lunch, dinner; closed Sun and Mon lunch 🚇 Faidherbe Chaligy

Au Pied de Cochon (€€)

Traditional 'Les Halles' restaurant; try the pig's trotters and onion soup.
✉ 6 rue Coquillère, 75001 ☎ 01 40 13 77 00; www.pieddecochon.com
🕐 24 hours 🚇 Châtelet Les Halles

Bar à Huîtres (€–€€)

Fashionable seafood brasserie.
✉ 33 boulevard Beaumarchais, 75003 ☎ 01 48 87 98 92; www.lebarahuitres.com 🕐 Lunch, dinner, open until 2am 🚇 Bastille

Brasserie Flo (€–€€)

1900-style Alsatian inn specializing in choucroute (sauerkraut) and seafood.
✉ 7 Cour des Petites Ecuries, 75010 ☎ 01 47 70 13 59; www.flobrasseries.com 🕐 Lunch, dinner 🚇 Château d'Eau

Caveau François Villon (€)

An attractive bistro in 15th-century cellars. Live music is played at night.
✉ 64 rue de l'Arbre Sec, 75001 ☎ 01 42 36 10 92 🕐 Lunch, dinner; closed Mon and Sat lunch, Sun 🚇 Louvre-Rivoli

Le Dôme du Marais (€€)
Imaginative cuisine based on fresh seasonal produce; historic surroundings.

✉ 53 bis rue des Francs-Bourgeois, 75004 ☎ 01 42 74 54 17 🕐 Lunch, dinner; closed Sun and Mon Ⓜ Hôtel de Ville

Le Dos de la Baleine (€)
Typical Marais restaurant with undressed-stone walls; innovative cuisine.

✉ 40 rue des Blancs-Manteaux, 75004 ☎ 01 42 72 38 98 🕐 Lunch, dinner; closed Sat lunch and Mon Ⓜ Rambuteau

Pharamond (€€)
Traditional food from Normandy, such as Caen-style tripe with cider, served in an historic listed building with an extravagant art nouveau interior.

✉ 24 rue de la Grande-Truanderie, 75001 ☎ 01 40 28 45 18; www.le-pharamond.com 🕐 Lunch, dinner; closed Sun Ⓜ Les Halles

Piccolo Teatro (€)
Refreshing and inspired selection of vegetarian dishes. Try the excellent soups.

✉ 6 rue des Ecouffes, 75004 ☎ 01 42 72 17 79 🕐 Lunch, dinner; closed Christmas Ⓜ St-Paul

La Poule au Pot (€€)
A bistro maintaining the traditions of Les Halles.

✉ 9 rue Vauvilliers, 75001 ☎ 01 42 36 32 96 🕐 Dinner; open until 6am; closed Mon Ⓜ Louvre Rivoli, Châtelet-les-Halles

Le Rouge Gorge (€€)
Delightful wine bar with lots of atmosphere.

✉ 8 rue St-Paul, 75004 ☎ 01 48 04 75 89 🕐 Lunch, dinner; closed Sun dinner Ⓜ St-Paul

Terminus Nord (€€)

A 1920s-style brasserie near the Gare du Nord; the speciality is duck foie gras with apple and raisins, seafood.

✉ 23 rue de Dunkerque, 75010 ☎ 01 42 85 05 15; www.terminusnord.com
🕐 Lunch, dinner 🚇 Gare du Nord

Le Vieux Bistrot (€€)

Facing the north side of Notre-Dame; traditional French cooking.

✉ 14 rue du Cloître-Notre-Dame, 75004 ☎ 01 43 54 18 95 🕐 Lunch, dinner
🚇 Cité

SHOPPING

ART, ANTIQUES AND HANDICRAFTS
Viaduc des Arts

Disused railway viaduct housing beneath its arches workshops and exhibitions displaying art and handicrafts.

✉ 9–129 avenue Daumesnil, 75012 🚇 Bastille, Ledru-Rollin, Reuilly-Diderot

Village Saint-Paul

A group of small antiques dealers established between rue Saint-Paul and rue Charlemagne.

✉ Le Marais, 75004 🚇 Saint-Paul, Pont-Marie, Sully-Morland

CHILDREN'S SHOP
Agnès B Enfant

Smart children's clothes by the fashionable designer.

✉ 2 rue du Jour, 75001 ☎ 01 40 39 96 88 🚇 Les Halles

DEPARTMENT STORES
Bazar de l'Hôtel de Ville

Known as the BHV, this store is famous for its huge do-it-yourself department, which claims to be the place to find what you can't find anywhere else!

✉ 52–64 rue de Rivoli, 75001 ☎ 01 42 74 90 00 🚇 Hôtel de Ville

Samaritaine
It lacks the stylishness of the boulevard Haussmann's stores but it offers a splendid view of Paris from the rooftop Toupary bistro.
✉ 19 rue de la Monnaie, 75001 ☎ 01 40 41 20 20 🚇 Pont Neuf

MARKET
Carreau du Temple
Covered market specializing in leather and second-hand clothes.
✉ 75003 🕓 Tue–Fri 9–1.30, Sat 9–6, Sun 9–2 🚇 Temple, Arts et Métiers

MISCELLANEOUS GIFTS
Agatha
Fashion jewellery shop.
✉ 99 rue de Rivoli, 75001 ☎ 01 42 96 03 09 🚇 Châtelet

Sic Amor
Fashion jewellery and accessories.
✉ 20 rue du Pont Louis-Philippe, 75004 ☎ 01 42 76 02 37 🚇 Pont-Marie

SHOPPING CENTRE
Forum des Halles
Underground shopping centre on several floors including chain-store fashion boutiques and the new Forum des Créateurs for young designers; also a huge FNAC store.
✉ 1–7 rue Pierre Lescot, 75001 🚇 Les Halles; RER Châtelet-Les Halles

ENTERTAINMENT

CONCERT VENUE
Théâtre du Châtelet
See page 73.

NIGHTCLUBS AND BARS
Les Bains Douches
Hip rendezvous of models and VIPs, with different styles of music.
✉ 7 rue du Bourg-l'Abbé, 75003 ☎ 01 48 87 01 80 🚇 Etienne Marcel

La Chapelle des Lombards

Salsa and Afro music; live shows mid-week.

✉ 19 rue de Lappe, 75011 ☎ 01 43 57 24 24 🚇 Bastille

La Casbah

See page 73.

Le Cithéa

High-quality live music, disco, jazz, funk, afro, soul. Stays open till late.

✉ 114 rue Oberkampf, 75011 ☎ 01 40 21 70 95; www.cithea.com
🚇 Oberkampf

SPORT

Piscine des Halles

Situated on Level 3 of Les Halles complex, this municipal sports centre has a 50m-long (164ft) underground swimming pool.

✉ 10 place de la Rotonde, 75001 ☎ 01 42 36 98 44 🚇 Les Halles

Hippodrome de Vincennes

Trotting races; Prix d'Amérique in late January.

✉ 2 route de la Ferme, 75012 ☎ 01 49 77 17 17 🚇 Château de Vincennes

Palais Omnisports de Paris Bercy (POPB)

Around 150 international sporting events every year, from athletics and tennis to horse jumping and basketball. Also hosts rock concerts and classical operas.

✉ 8 boulevard de Bercy, 75012 ☎ 01 40 02 60 60; www.bercy.fr
🚇 Bercy

Montmartre

**This unassuming village overlooking Paris
became a myth during the 19th century, when it was
taken over by artists and writers attracted by its
picturesque surroundings and bohemian way of life.
La 'Butte' (the mound) managed to retain its village
atmosphere and now that the area has become a major
tourist attraction, an undefinable nostalgia lingers on,
perpetuating Montmartre's magic appeal.**

In its heyday, the district was the favourite haunt and home of
many famous artists. They met in cafés and in cabarets such as
the Moulin-Rouge (1889), whose singers and dancers acquired
world-wide fame through Toulouse-Lautrec's paintings and
posters. Today it is a mix of teeming tourist traps such as place
du Tertre and Sacre-Coeur, and quiet cobbled enclaves, with
whitewashed cottages and more than a hint of its former
'village' atmosphere.

AU LAPIN AGILE

At the corner of rue St-Vincent, watch out for the Montmartre vineyard and the Au Lapin Agile nightclub, the rendezvous of young artists and writers in the early 1900s (➤ 165).

✚ 27R ✉ 22 rue des Saules, 75018 ☎ 01 46 06 85 87 🚇 Tue–Sun 9.15pm–2am ✋ Expensive (includes a drink) 🚇 Lamarck-Caulaincourt

BATEAU-LAVOIR

Halfway up the hill of Montmartre, a wooden construction known as the Bateau-Lavoir, where, among others, Picasso, Braque and Juan Gris had their studios, was the modest birthplace of Cubism. Destroyed by fire in 1970, it has since been rebuilt.

✚ 26R ✉ 13 place Emile-Goudeau, 75018 🚇 Abbesses

ESPACE MONTMARTRE SALVADOR DALÍ

A collection of more than 300 quirky works by the flamboyant artist Salvador Dalí (1904–89) are on display here, forming the biggest Dalí collection in France. It includes sculptures, illustrations, lithographs and some of his less familiar paintings.

✚ 27R ✉ 9–11 rue Poulbot, 75018 ☎ 01 42 64 40 10 🚇 Daily 10–6 ✋ Moderate 🚇 Abbesses

LA VILLETTE

See pages 54–55.

MARCHÉ AUX PUCES DE ST-OUEN

This is said to be the largest flea market in the world, covering 7ha (17 acres) just north of Montmartre (➤ 164). More than 2,000 stalls are grouped into 13 different *marchés*, each with its own specialities, from bric-à-brac and second-hand clothes to pricey antiques and wacky 1970s furniture. Be prepared to haggle, pay in cash and keep watch out for pickpockets.

✚ 28T (off map) ✉ Streets around rue des Rosiers, 75018 🚇 Sat–Mon 9.30–6 (some stands open earlier) 🚇 Porte de Clignancourt, Garibaldi

MONTMARTRE, CIMETIÈRE DE

Montmartre's cemetery is the most famous graveyard in Paris after Père-Lachaise (➤ 144–145). It is filled with the graves of the famous, such as composers Hector Berlioz and Jacques Offenbach, artists Edgar Degas and Jean Honoré Fragonard, writers Heinrich Heine and Émile Zola (whose remains were removed to the Panthéon), and film director François Truffaut. You can pick up a plan of the graves at the main entrance, and there are also guided tours at certain times.

➕ 25R ✉ 20 avenue Rachel, 75018 ☎ 01 53 42 36 30 🕐 Mid-Mar to early Nov Mon–Fri 8–6, Sat 8.30–6, Sun 9–6; early Nov to mid-Mar Mon–Fri 8–5.30, Sat 8.30–5.30, Sun 9–5.30 (last entry 15 mins before closing)
🚇 Place de Clichy/Blanche

MOULIN DE LA GALETTE

The Moulin de la Galette, one of Montmartre's two remaining windmills was the venue for a popular ball that inspired Renoir's famous painting: *Le Bal du Moulin de la Galette*, now in the Musée d'Orsay (➤ 48–49). Built in 1622, the 'Biscuit Windmill' was named after the delicious galette biscuits made here using flour from the mill.

✚ 26R ✉ Rue Tholozé, 75018 (privately owned) 🚇 Abbesses

MOULIN-ROUGE

In its heyday, the district was the favourite haunt and home of many famous artists. They met in cafés and in cabarets such as the Moulin-Rouge ('Red Windmill'), whose singers and dancers acquired world-wide fame through Toulouse-Lautrec's paintings and posters. It was never actually a windmill but was launched as a cabaret venue in 1889. Shows are still performed here today, but at a price (➤ 165).

www.moulinrouge.fr

✚ 25Q ✉ 82 boulevard de Clichy, 75018 ☎ 01 53 09 82 82 🎭 Spectacles nightly at 9 and 11. Combined dinner and show at 7pm 💷 Expensive 🚇 Blanche

MUSIQUE, MUSÉE DE LA

Housed within the vast Cité de la Musique (➤ 55), the museum presents a permanent exhibition consisting of some 900 musical instruments dating from the Renaissance to the present day, as well as works of art and objets d'art inspired in some way by music. Regular concerts and lectures and various cultural events take place in the 230-seat auditorium.

✚ 28Q (off map) ✉ 221 avenue Jean-Jaurès, 75019 ☎ 01 44 84 44 84 🕐 Tue–Sat 12–6, Sun 10–6 💷 Moderate 🚇 Porte de Pantin 🚌 75, 151, PC

SACRÉ-COEUR, BASILIQUE DU

The white domes and campaniles of this neo-Byzantine basilica stand out against the skyline, high above the rooftops of the capital. Its construction at the top of Montmartre was undertaken as a sign of national reconciliation and hope after the bitter defeat suffered by France in the 1870 war against Prussia. Funds were raised by public subscription and work started in 1875, but the basilica took nearly 45 years to build and was inaugurated only in 1919, at the end of another war!

The view over Paris from the terrace in front of the building is breathtaking; an impressive number of steps leads down to the place St-Pierre; from the dome, an even more stunning panoramic view stretches for 50km (31 miles) around the city. The interior of the basilica is profusely decorated with mosaics.

www.sacre-coeur-montmartre.com

✚ 27R ✉ Place du Parvis du Sacré-Coeur, 75018 ☎ 01 53 41 89 00 🌐 Basilica: daily 6am–11pm; dome and crypt: daily 9–6 (7 in summer) ✋ Basilica: free; dome and crypt: inexpensive 🚇 Abbesses (from here walk along rue Yvonne Le Tac, then take funicular or walk up steps) 🚌 30, 31, 80, 85, Montmartrobus ❓ Shops

ST-PIERRE, ÉGLISE

Just to the west of Sacré-Coeur is the diminutive 12th-century church of St-Pierre-de-Montmartre, consecrated in 1147 and one of Paris's oldest churches. This lovely, peaceful church is all that remains of the Benedictine abbey of Montmartre.

✚ 27R ✉ 2 rue du Mont-Cenis, 75018 🚇 Abbesses

TERTRE, PLACE DU

The whole of place du Tertre (*tertre* means hillock), one of the most hectic tourist spots in Paris, is filled with easels and would-be artists, all trying to sell their work or sketch you. (Note you are not obliged to pay if they produce an unsolicited portrait of you.) For most of the year it bustles with crowds who come to eat and

people-watch in this tiny, café-bordered square at the heart of Montmartre, but during winter, it manages to retain its rural atmosphere.

At No 6, on one corner of the square, you will find La Mère Catherine (☎ 01 46 06 32 69), an unassuming little bistro dating from the Napoleonic era and very popular with the Russian troops who occupied the city in 1814. They were in the habit of banging the table and shouting 'bistro!' (meaning 'quick!') which gave rise to the name for such unpretentious eating places. Here you can occasionally sample Montmartre's own wine made with grapes from the area's one surviving vineyard.

✚ 27R ✉ Place du Tertre, 75018 🚇 Abbesses

VIEUX MONTMARTRE, MUSÉE DE

The Musée de Vieux Montmartre has works and memorabilia by the artists who lived here, and the narrow cobbled streets of the 'Butte' still have some amazing sights to offer, including a vineyard in the picturesque rue des Saules and two windmills in the twisting rue Lepic.

✚ 27R ✉ 12 rue Cortot, 75018 🕐 Tue–Sun 11–6. Closed 1 Jan,1 May, 25 Dec ✋ Inexpensive 🚇 Lamarck-Caulaincourt 🖼 Exhibitions, bookshop

HOTELS

Hôtel des Arts (€)
Close to Sacré-Coeur and the rue des Abbesses, this comfortable hotel has a warm interior with fine furniture. There is also parking nearby.

✉ 5 rue de Tholozé, 75018 ☎ 01 46 06 30 52; www.hotel-des-arts.net
🚇 Abbesses, Blanche

Hôtel le Bouquet de Montmartre (€)
The rooms in this comfortable hotel may have limited facilities, but there are pleasing little features such as alcoves by the beds and candelabra wall lamps. Enjoy breakfast in the beautiful dining room.

✉ 1 rue Durantin, 75018 ☎ 01 46 06 87 54; www.paris-montmartre-hotel.com 🚇 Abbesses

Hôtel Regyn's Montmartre (€–€€)
There are views of Sacré-Coeur from some of the rooms here, while others look out over the delightful place des Abbesses.

✉ 11 place des Abbesses, 75018 ☎ 01 42 54 45 21;
www.regynsmontmartre.com 🚇 Abbesses

Hôtel Prima Lepic (€)
The quietest rooms in this tastefully furnished hotel overlook an inner courtyard, while those facing rue Lepic give a fascinating view of bustling Parisian life. Sacré-Coeur and the Moulin Rouge are both a short walk away.

✉ 29 rue Lepic, 75018 ☎ 01 46 06 44 64; www.hotel-paris-lepic.com
🚇 Blanche/Abbesses

Terrass Hôtel (€€€)
The comfortable, family-run Terrass, at the foot of the Butte Montmartre, has a 7th-floor restaurant (May–Sep only) which offers a superb view of the city. Rooms and suites are available.

✉ 12 rue Joseph-de-Maistre 75018 ☎ 01 44 92 34 14; www.terrass-hotel.com 🚇 Blanche/Place-de-Clichy

Tim Hôtel Montmartre (€€)

In the old part of Montmartre, with lovely views; attention to detail makes it a comfortable if simple place to stay.

✉ 11 rue Ravignan, 75018 ☎ 01 42 55 74 79; www.timhotel.com
🕐 All year 🚇 Abbesses

RESTAURANTS

Au Pied du Sacré-Coeur (€–€€)

The cuisine at this restaurant, situated at the foot of Sacré-Coeur, ranges from traditonal dishes, such as grilled steak in pepper sauce to more exotic fare, such as poultry stuffed with prawns.

✉ Square Caulaincourt, 75018 ☎ 01 46 15 26 🕐 Tue–Sun noon–3, 7.30–midnight 🚇 Lamarck-Caulaincourt

Au Rendezvous des Chauffeurs (€)

This popular, unpretentious restaurant, popular with local diners, serves home-style cooking at reasonable prices, from juicy steaks with fat *frites* to kidneys, *andouilles* (chitterling sausage) and steak tartare.

✉ 11 rue des Portes-Blanches, 75018 ☎ 01 42 64 04 17 🕐 Thu–Tue noon–2.30, 7.30–10.30. Closed Aug, Thu in summer 🚇 Marcadet-Poissonniers

Beauvilliers (€€–€€€)

See page 62.

Brasserie Wepler (€€)

Brasserie Wepler, with its late 19th-century ambience, offers a classic menu that includes an exceptional seafood platter as well as other familiar dishes, such as French onion soup, bouillabaisse, duck foie gras, *choucroute*, steak tartare and grilled sirloin. Leave room for one of the outstanding desserts.

✉ 14 place de Clichy, 75018 ☎ 01 45 22 53 24; www.wepler.com 🕐 Daily noon–1am 🚇 Place de Clichy

Chez Toinette (€)

Chez Toinette is open only for dinner. The beef carpaccio seasoned with ground nutmeg is a popular starter, then choose from one of the main courses of fish, meat or game. The desserts are exceptional. No credit cards; reservations advisable, especially on Fridays and Saturdays.

✉ 20 rue Germain-Pilon, 75018 ☎ 01 42 54 44 36 🕐 Tue–Sat 8pm–11pm; closed Aug 🚇 Abbesses

L'Etrier (€–€€)

The traditional French cuisine here is good value for money. Reserve a table in advance.

✉ 154 rue Lamarck, 75018 ☎ 01 42 29 14 01 🕐 Lunch, dinner; closed Mon, Sun and Aug 🚇 Guy Môquet

Pavillon Puebla (€€–€€€)

In the lovely parc des Buttes Chaumont; elegant Napoleon III décor; the speciality is lobster à la catalane.

✉ Parc des Buttes Chaumont (entrance on the corner of avenue Bolivar and rue Botzaris), 75019 ☎ 01 42 08 92 62 🕐 Lunch, dinner; closed Sun and Mon 🚇 Buttes Chaumont

Le Poulbot Gourmet (€€)

With scenes of old Montmartre on the walls, this lovely little restaurant has a mouthwatering menu that changes two or three times a year, and might include Barbary duck with baby turnips or lamb noisettes with thyme jus.

✉ 39 rue Lamarck, 75018 ☎ 01 46 06 86 00 🕐 Mon–Sat 12.30–2, 7.30–10; closed Sun Jun–Sep and 2 weeks in Aug 🚇 Lamarck

Le Virage Lepic (€)

The food in this cosy bistro on one of lower Montmartre's most atmospheric streets, is utterly delicious, and the wine list includes an excellent house champagne. You can sit outside in summer. Reserve in advance.

✉ 61 rue Lepic, 75018 ☎ 01 42 52 46 79 🕐 Wed–Mon 7pm–11pm 🚇 Blanche, Abbesses

SHOPPING

FOOD AND DRINK
Epicerie Collignon
This traditional grocery shop was made famous in the 2001 film *Amelie*.

✉ 56 rue des Trois Frères, 75018 ☎ 01 42 64 86 30 🚇 Abbesses

FASHION AND ACCESSORIES
Bonnie Cox
This Montmartre boutique is popular with trendy teenagers.

✉ 38 rue des Abbesses, 75018 ☎ 01 42 54 95 68 🚇 Abbesses

Loorica
Loorica, in an up-and-coming district, has attracted young, talented designers who create futuristic bags for discerning people.

✉ 8bis rue des Gardes, 75018 ☎ 01 44 92 01 26 🚇 Barbés-Rochechouart

Tati
Tati is known for its cut-price fashions.

✉ 4 boulevard de Rochechouart, 75018 ☎ 01 55 29 50 00 🕐 Closed Sun
🚇 Barbès-Rochechouart

MARKETS
Marché aux Puces de Saint-Ouen
The largest flea market in Paris. Everything you can think of is for sale. Prices are often inflated, be prepared to bargain (➤ 154).

✉ Streets around rue des Rosiers, 75018 🕐 Sat–Mon 9.30–6 (some stands open earlier) 🚇 Porte de Clignancourt, Garibaldi

Marché Saint-Pierre
Huge discount store at the foot of Sacre-Coeur selling high-quality fabrics, tapestries and clothing.

✉ 2 rue Charles Nodier, 75018 ☎ 01 46 06 92 25; www.marche-saint-pierre.fr 🕐 Mon 1.30–6.30, Tue–Sat 10–6.30 🚇 Anvers

ENTERTAINMENT

CABARET
Au Lapin Agile
This Montmartre cabaret makes a great night out with its mix of
popular music and sharp-edged repartee (➤ 154).
✉ 22 rue des Saules, 75018 ☎ 01 46 06 85 87; www.au-lapin-agile.com
🕒 Tue–Sun 9.15pm–2am 🚇 Lamarck-Caulaincourt

Moulin-Rouge
Undoubtedly the most famous cabaret of them all! The Moulin
Rouge's show still includes impressive displays of French can-can
(➤ 157).
✉ 82 boulevard de Clichy, 75018 ☎ 01 53 09 82 82 🚇 Blanche

CONCERT VENUES
Cité de la Musique
This temple of classical music regularly sets new trends with
special commissions.
✉ 221 avenue Jean Jaurès, 75019 ☎ 01 44 84 44 84; www.cite-musique.fr
🚇 Porte de Pantin

NIGHTCLUBS
Folies Pigalle
The mid-20s crowd that comes to this nightclub in Paris's red-light
district. grooves to the sound of house in a highly charged
atmosphere.
✉ 11 place Pigalle, 75009 ☎ 01 48 78 55 25; www.folies-pigalle.com
🚇 Pigalle

Le Divan du Monde
For a great atmosphere and reasonably priced drinks, try Le Divan
du Monde. This small and inviting concert venue runs theme
nights, with an emphasis on world music.
✉ 75 rue des Martyrs, 75018 ☎ 01 44 92 77 66; www.divandumonde.com
🕒 Daily 7pm–7am 🚇 Pigalle, Anvers, Abbesses

Excursions

'Île de France', as the Paris region is called, means the heart of France; and this is exactly what it has always been and still is, the very core of the country, a prosperous and dynamic region, inhabited by one French person in five, with Paris in its centre. Roads, motorways and international railway lines converge on this central region, which has become one of Europe's main crossroads, with two major international airports.

Besides its tremendous vitality, the Île de France offers visitors attractive natural assets, a rich cultural heritage and a gentle way of life. The countryside is domestic rather than spectacular, graced by picturesque villages, country inns, manor houses, historic castles, abbeys, cathedrals and beautiful parks and gardens.

CHANTILLY, CHÂTEAU DE

The Château de Chantilly houses the Musée Condé, named after one of its most distinguished owners, Le Grand Condé. The 16th-century Petit Château contains the 'Princes' apartments' and a library full of precious illuminated manuscripts, including the 15th-century *Les Très Riches Heures du Duc de Berry*; the Grand Château, destroyed during the Revolution and rebuilt in Renaissance style at the end of the 19th century, houses a magnificent collection of paintings by Raphael, Clouet, Ingres, Corot and Delacroix, as well as porcelain and jewellery.

Facing the famous racecourse, the 18th-century stables have been turned into the Musée Vivant du Cheval, illustrating the various crafts, jobs and sports connected with horses.

www.chateaudechantilly.com

✉ 40km (25 miles) north of Paris. BP 70243, 60631 Chantilly Cedex
☎ Château and Musée Conde: 03 44 62 62 62; Musée Vivant du Cheval: 03 44 57 40 40 🕓 Chateau: Mar–Oct Wed–Mon 10–6, Nov–Feb Wed–Mon 10.30–12.45, 2–5. Musée du Cheval: Mar–Oct daily 10.30–6.30; Nov–Feb daily 2–6 ✋ Moderate 🍴 Near the station (€) 🚇 Gare du Nord to Chantilly-Gouvieux

DISNEYLAND® RESORT PARIS

Disneyland® Resort Paris offers fantasy, humour, *joie de vivre*, excitement and the latest technological devices to ensure that your visit is a memorable one. Besides Disneyland® Park and Walt Disney Studios® Park, there is a whole range of 'typically' American hotels to tempt you to stay on for a day or two.

www.disneylandparis.com

✉ 30km (19 miles) east of Paris. BP100 77777 Marne-la-Vallée ☎ UK: 08705 03 03 03; in France: 01 60 30 60 30 🕓 Varies with the season ✋ Moderate
🍴 Inside the park (€–€€€) 🚇 RER A Marne-la-Vallée/Chessy

FONTAINEBLEAU, CHÂTEAU DE

A fountain or spring, now in the Jardin Anglais, is at the origin of this splendid royal residence, which started out as a hunting pavilion at the heart of a vast forest. It was François I who made Fontainebleau into the beautiful palace it is today, although it was later remodelled by successive monarchs. The imposing horseshoe staircase decorating the main façade was the scene of Napoleon I's moving farewell to his faithful guard in 1814. Beyond this building lies the Etang des Carpes (carp pool) with a lovely pavilion in its centre, and further on the formal French gardens. The oldest part of the palace, including the keep of the medieval castle, surrounds the Cour Ovale. The State Apartments contain paintings, furniture and objets d'art, the fine coffered ceiling of the Salle de Bal and frescoes in the Galerie François I.

✉ 65km (40 miles) southeast of Paris. 77300 Fontainebleau ☎ 60 71 50 70 🕐 Wed–Sun 9.30–12.30, 2–5 (reduced hours Sep–Jun). Closed 1 Jan, 1 May, 25 Dec 💷 Moderate 🍴 In the town nearby (€–€€€) 🚇 Gare de Lyon to Fontainebleau-Avon and 🚌 A or B ❓ Guided tour, shops

FRANCE MINIATURE

This open-air museum comprises a huge three-dimensional map of France on which 166 miniature historic monuments have been arranged. There are models of the Tour Eiffel, Sacré Coeur, Mont-St-Michel, the pont du Gard and Gallo-Roman arenas, as well as many beautiful castles, all made to a scale of 1:30. Here and there, a typical French village focuses on ordinary daily life.

✉ 25km (15 miles) west of Paris. 25 route du Mesnil, 78990 Elancourt ☎ 01 30 62 40 78 🕐 Apr–early Nov 10–6 (7 in Jul and Aug); last admission 1 hour before closing 💷 Moderate 🍴 Two restaurants (€–€€) 🚇 Gare Montparnasse ❓ Audiovisual show, outdoor activities

PARC ASTÉRIX

This theme park is based on the comic adventures of a friendly little Gaul named Astérix and his companions, who are determined to resist the Roman invaders. The story became famous world-wide through a series of strip cartoons by Goscinny and Uderzo, which have since been translated into many languages.

Inside the park, visitors are invited to share Astérix's adventures as they wander through the Gauls' Village, the Roman City and Ancient Greece, travel on the impressive roller-coaster of the Great Lake and journey back and forth in time along the rue de Paris! ✉ 30km (19 miles) north of Paris. BP 8, 60128 Plailly ☎ 03 44 62 34 04 🕐 Early Apr–early Sep 9.30 or 10–6 or 7. Closed some days outside peak season of mid-Jun to Aug ✋ Moderate 🍴 Several choices (€–€€) 🚇 RER B3 from Châtelet or Gare du Nord to Roissy-Charles-de-Gaulle 1 then G Courriers Île-de-France every half hour ❓ Gift shops, picnic areas, pushchair (stroller) rental

SAINT-CLOUD, PARC DE

This beautiful park, on the outskirts of Paris, extends over a vast hilly area overlooking the Seine. The castle designed by Jules-Hardouin Mansart for Louis XIV's brother, was destroyed by fire in 1870 and razed to the ground in 1891. It had been Bonaparte's favourite official residence when he was consul of the Republic.

The park was designed by Le Nôtre. At the top the site of the former castle is now a terrace offering lovely views of the capital. Nearby is the Jardin du Trocadéro, an English-style garden with an ornamental pool and an aviary. There are many shaded alleyways offering delightful walks through the 460ha (1,136-acre) park.

✉ 11km (7 miles) west of Paris. 92210 Saint-Cloud ☎ 01 41 12 02 90
🕐 Daily 7.30am–8.50pm (7.50pm Nov–Feb, 9.50 May–Aug) 🖐 Free
🍴 Cafés (€) 🚊 Pont de Saint-Cloud

SAINT-GERMAIN-EN-LAYE

The historic city of Saint-Germain-en-Laye clusters round its royal castle, once the favourite residence of Louis XIV. François I commissioned the present Château Vieux (Old Castle) and retained Saint-Louis's chapel and the 14th-century square keep, now surmounted by a campanile. Le Nôtre later designed the gardens and the magnificent 2,400m-long (7,872ft) Grande Terrasse. The Sun King stayed in Saint-Germain for many years and during that time private mansions were built around the castle for members of his court. When the court moved to Versailles in 1682, the castle was somewhat neglected but it was eventually restored by Napoleon III and turned into the Musée des Antiquités Nationales, which houses interesting archaeological collections illustrating life in France from earliest times to the Middle Ages.

✉ 23km (14 miles) west of Paris.

Château de Saint-Germain-en-Laye

✉ BP 3030, 78105 Saint-Germain-en-Laye Cedex ☎ 01 39 10 13 00
🕐 Wed–Mon 9–5.15. Closed some public hols 🖐 Inexpensive 🚊 RER Saint-Germain-en-Laye ❓ Guided tours, shops

VAUX-LE-VICOMTE, CHÂTEAU DE

This architectural gem cost its owner, Nicolas Fouquet, his freedom and eventually his life. Fouquet had commissioned the best artists of his time: Le Vau for the building, Le Brun for the decoration and Le Nôtre for the gardens. Louis XIV was invited to a reception given for the inauguration of the castle in 1661. He did not take kindly to being outshone: Fouquet was arrested and spent the rest of his life in prison, while Louis commissioned the same artists to build him an even more splendid castle, Versailles.

The castle stands on a terrace overlooking magnificent gardens featuring canals, pools and fountains.

✉ 51km (32 miles) southeast of Paris. Domaine de Vaux-le-Vicomte, 77950 Maincy ☎ 01 64 14 41 90 🕐 Late Mar to mid-Nov Mon–Fri 10–1, 2–6, Sat, Sun 10–6. Candlelit visits: early May to mid-Oct Sat 8pm–midnight (also Fri Jul–Aug) ✋ Expensive 🚆 Gare de Lyon to Melun then taxi

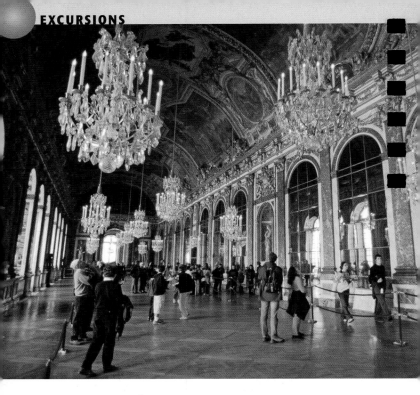

VERSAILLES, CHÂTEAU DE

The physical expression of a king's superego, Versailles turned out to be one of the most splendid castles in the world through the genius of the artists who built and decorated it. What began as a modest hunting lodge became the seat of government and political centre of France for over a hundred years. A town grew up around the castle to accommodate the court. Several thousand men worked on the castle for 50 years, thousands of trees were transplanted, and 3,000 people could live in it.

The castle is huge (680m/2,230ft long) and it is impossible to see everything in the course of one visit. Aim for the first floor where the State Apartments are, including the famous Galerie des Glaces, as well as the Official Apartments and the Private

Apartments of the royal couple, situated on either side of the marble courtyard. The north wing contains the two-floor Chapelle St-Louis built by Mansart and the Opéra, added later, by Gabriel.

The focal point of the park is the Bassin d'Apollon, a magnificent ornamental pool with a bronze sculpture in its centre representing Apollo's chariot coming out of the water. Two smaller castles, Le Grand Trianon and Le Petit Trianon, are also worth a visit, and Le Hameau, Marie-Antoinette's retreat, offers a delightful contrast.

www.chateauversailles.fr

✉ 20km (12.5 miles) southwest of Paris. 78000 Versailles ☎ 01 30 83 78 00

🕓 Château: Tue–Sun 9–5.30 (6.30 in summer); closed some public hols. Trianons: daily noon–5.30 (6.30 in summer). Parc: daily 7–5.30 (up to 9.30pm depending on season; from 8am winter) ceremonies 🖐 Moderate
🍴 Cafeteria (€) and restaurant (€€)
🚇 Gare St-Lazare to Versailles Rive Droite

in and around the Forêt de Fontainebleau

The forest of Fontainebleau extends over a vast area along the left bank of the Seine, to the southeast of the capital.

Start at the Porte d'Orléans and follow the A6 motorway towards Evry and Lyon. Leave at the Fontainebleau exit and continue on the N37 for 7km (4 miles); turn right to Barbizon.

This village gave its name to a group of landscape painters who settled there in the mid-19th century. They were joined later by some of the future Impressionists: Renoir, Sisley and Monet. The **Auberge Ganne**, which they decorated with their paintings, is now a museum.

Leave Barbizon towards Fontainebleau.

Take time to visit the château (➤ 170), or at least the park, and to stroll around the town.

Drive southeast along the D58 , bearing left at the Y-junction. Turn right onto the Route Ronde (D301).

This scenic route takes you through the forest and offers many possibilities for walking and cycling.

Turn left on the D409 to Milly-la-Forêt.

This small town nestling round an imposing covered market is a traditional centre for growing medicinal plants. The Cyclop (1km/0.5 miles north) is a monumental modern sculpture which took 20 years to complete.

Take the D372 for 3.5km (2 miles); bear left for Courances.

The **Château de Courances** looks delightful, set like a jewel in a magnificent park designed by Le Nôtre, with pools, canals and small waterfalls.

Return to the main road and continue for 5km (3 miles), then rejoin the motorway back to Paris.

Distance 143km (89 miles)
Time 7–9 hours depending on length of visits
Start/end point Porte d'Orléans
Lunch Le Caveau des Ducs ✉ 24 rue de Ferrare, 77300 Fontainebleau ☎ 01 64 22 05 05

Auberge Ganne
✉ 92 Grande Rue, 77630 Barbizon ☎ 01 60 66 22 27 🕐 Apr–Sep Wed–Mon 10–12.30, 2–5 💷 Moderate

Château de Courances
✉ 91240 Milly-la-Forêt ☎ 01 40 62 07 71 🕐 Apr–Oct Sat, Sun and public hols 2–6.30 💷 Moderate ❓ Guided tours

VINCENNES, CHÂTEAU DE

This austere castle, situated on the eastern outskirts of Paris, was a royal residence from the Middle Ages to the mid-17th century. Inside the defensive wall, there are in fact two castles: the 50m-high (164ft) keep (currently undergoing repair) built in the 14th century, which later held political prisoners, philosophers, soldiers, ministers and churchmen; and the two classical pavilions built by Le Vau for Cardinal Mazarin in 1652, Le Pavillon de la Reine, where Anne d'Autriche, mother of Louis XIV lived, and Le Pavillon du Roi, where Mazarin died in 1661. The Chapelle Royale, started by Saint-Louis and completed by François I, stands in the main courtyard.

✉ 6km (4 miles) east of Paris. Avenue de Paris, 94300 Vincennes ☎ 01 48 08 31 20 ⏰ Daily 10–noon, 1.15–5 (6 in summer). Closed 1 Jan, 1 May, 1 Nov, 11 Nov, 25 Dec ✋ Inexpensive 🚇 Métro: Château de Vincennes ❓ Guided tours, shops

HOTELS

CHANTILLY
Château de Montvillargenne (€€–€€€)
Large mansion in vast own grounds; covered swimming pool, sauna, sports facilities.
✉ 1 avenue François Mathet, 60270 Gouvieux ☎ 03 44 62 37 37; www.chateaudemontvillargenne.com 🚇 Gare du Nord to Chantilly-Gouvieux

DISNEYLAND
Disney's Hotel Cheyenne® (€–€€)
Each of the hotels has its own authentic American theme; this one is self-explanatory.
☎ 01 60 45 62 00 🚇 RER Marne-la-Vallée/Chessy

FONTAINEBLEAU
Grand Hôtel de l'Aigle Noir (€€€)
Napoleon III-style decoration for this hotel facing the castle; fitness club, indoor swimming pool and very good restaurant.
✉ 27 place Napoléon Bonaparte, 77300 Fontainebleau ☎ 01 60 74 60 00; www.hotelaiglenoir.fr 🚇 Gare de Lyon to Fontainebleau-Avon

SAINT-GERMAIN-EN-LAYE
Pavillon Henri IV (€€–€€€)
Historic building near the famous Grande Terrasse; great views.
✉ 19–21 rue Thiers, 78100 Saint-Germain-en-Laye ☎ 01 39 10 15 15; www.pavillonhenri4.fr 🚇 RER Saint-Germain-en-Laye

VERSAILLES
Relais de Courlande (€)
An attractive converted 16th-century farmhouse offering hydrotherapy.
✉ 23 rue de la Division Leclerc, 78350 Les Loges-en-Josas ☎ 01 30 83 84 00 🚇 Gare Saint-Lazare to Versailles Rive Droite; RER C to Versailles Rive Gauche

RESTAURANTS

CHANTILLY
Château de la Tour (€€)
Refined cuisine and wood-panelled décor; terrace in summer.
✉ Chemin de la Chaussée, 60270 Gouvieux (1km/0.5 miles from Chantilly)
☎ 03 44 62 38 38 🕐 Lunch, dinner 🚆 Gare du Nord to Chantilly-Gouvieux

CONDÉ-STE-LIBIAIRE
La Vallée de la Marne (€–€€)
Peaceful setting; dining-room overlooks the garden on the banks
of the River Marne (3km/2 miles from Disneyland).
✉ 2 quai Marne, 77450 Condé-Ste-Libiaire ☎ 01 60 04 31 01 🕐 Lunch,
dinner; closed Mon dinner, Tue 🚆 RER A Marne-la-Vallée/Chessy

FONTAINEBLEAU
L'Atrium (€–€€)
Pizzeria in the town centre; attractive year-round terrace dining.
✉ 20 rue France, 77300 Fontainebleau ☎ 01 64 22 18 36 🕐 Lunch, dinner
🚆 Gare de Lyon to Fontainebleau-Avon then 🚌 A or B

Le Caveau des Ducs (€€)
Elegant restaurant in vaulted cellars; terrace in summer.
✉ 24 rue Ferrare, 77300 Fontainebleau ☎ 01 64 22 05 05 🕐 Lunch, dinner
🚆 Gare de Lyon to Fontainebleau-Avon then 🚌 A or B

SAINT-CLOUD
Quai Ouest (€€)
This 'Floating warehouse' serving appetizing fish and poultry
dishes is the place to go when the sun is out.
✉ 1200 quai Marcel Dassault, 92210 Saint-Cloud ☎ 01 46 02 35 54
🕐 Lunch, dinner 🚆 Gare Saint-Lazare to Saint-Cloud

SAINT-DENIS
Campanile Saint-Denis Basilique (€)
One of a chain of inn-style modern hotels serving good cuisine.
✉ 14 rue Jean-Jaurès, 93200 Saint-Denis ☎ 01 48 20 74 31 🕐 Lunch,
dinner 🚇 Métro Saint-Denis-Basilique

SAINT-GERMAIN-EN-LAYE
Ermitage des Loges (€€)
Reasonably priced cuisine with an emphasis on fish and seafood. Summer eating is in the garden.

✉ 11 avenue des Loges, 78100 Saint-Germain-en-Laye ☎ 01 39 21 50 90
🕐 Lunch, dinner 🚇 RER Saint-Germain-en-Laye

Feuillantine (€)
You will find tasty cuisine at moderate prices in this elegant commuterland setting close to the impressive château.

✉ 10 rue Louviers, 78100 Saint-Germain-en-Laye ☎ 01 34 51 04 24
🕐 Lunch, dinner 🚇 RER Saint-Germain-en-Laye

VAUX-LE-VICOMTE
La Mare au Diable (€€)
Lovely old 15th-century manor house with beams; terrace for summer meals.

✉ RN6, 77550 Melun-Sénart (10km/6 miles from Vaux-le-Vicomte) ☎ 01 64 10 20 90 🕐 Lunch, dinner; closed Mon all day, Tue and Sun dinner 🚇 Gare de Lyon to Melun

VERSAILLES
Le Boeuf à la Mode (€)
Old-fashioned brasserie with sunny terrace serving excellent duck and vegetable spaghettis.

✉ 4 rue au Pain, 78000 Versailles ☎ 01 39 50 31 99 🕐 Lunch, dinner
🚇 Gare Saint-Lazare to Versailles Rive-Droite; RER C to Versailles Rive Gauche

La Cuisine Bourgeoise (€€)
Tasty refined cuisine served in cosy surroundings; perfect place to stop on a day out to Versailles.

✉ 10 boulevard du Roi, 78000 Versailles ☎ 01 39 53 11 38 🕐 Lunch, dinner; closed Sat lunch, Sun, Mon and 3 weeks in Aug 🚇 Gare Saint-Lazare to Versailles Rive-Droite; RER C to Versailles Rive Gauche

SHOPPING

BARBIZON
Galerie d'Art Castiglione
One of more than 10 art galleries to be found in this popular artists' village.

✉ Grande rue, 77630 Barbizon ☎ 01 60 69 22 12

FONTAINEBLEAU
Boutique du Musée National de Fontainebleau
For history buffs fascinated by Napoleon I and European history at the beginning of the 19th century.

✉ Château de Fontainebleau, 77300 Fontainebleau ☎ 01 60 71 50 70
🚆 Gare de Lyon to Fontainebleau-Avon, then 🚌 A or B

SAINT-GERMAIN-EN-LAYE
Boutique du Musée des Antiquités Nationales
History books from prehistory to the early Middle Ages as well as reproductions of jewellery and various items from the museum's collections.

✉ Place du Château, 78100 Saint-Germain-en-Laye ☎ 01 39 10 13 22
🚆 RER Saint-Germain-en-Laye

Les Galeries de Saint-Germain
Close to the RER and the Château, 42 boutiques in les Galeries de Saint-Germain sell fashion, articles for the home and gifts; famous names include Chanel and Yves Saint-Laurent.

✉ 10 rue de la Salle, 78100 Saint-Germain-en-Laye ☎ 01 39 73 70 67
🕐 Closed Mon 🚆 RER Saint-Germain-en-Laye

VERSAILLES
Librairie-Boutique de l'Ancienne Comédie
There are 2,000 titles connected with the castle, its gardens and its history, many with information on 17th-and 18th-century architecture.

✉ Château de Versailles, passage des Princes, 78000 Versailles ☎ 01 30 83 76 90 🕐 May–Sep daily 9–6.30; Oct–Apr daily 9–5.30 🚆 Gare Saint-Lazare to Versailles Rive Droite; RER C to Versailles Rive Gauche

ENTERTAINMENT

CONCERT
Soirées Musicales au Château de Versailles
Concerts of baroque music on Thursdays and Saturdays, from
November to June in the Opera house and the Royal Chapel.
Information from the Centre de Musique Baroque de Versailles.
✉ 22 avenue de Paris, 78003 Versailles ☎ 01 39 20 78 10

SHOWS
Disneyland Paris
Buffalo Bill's Wild West Show
A fast moving dinner-show in the company of Buffalo Bill.
☎ Bookings: 01 60 45 71 00

Vaux-le-Vicomte
Visites aux Chandelles
Tours of the Château de Vaux-le-Vicomte by candlelight take place
every Saturday night from early May to mid-October.
✉ Château de Vaux-le-Vicomte, 77950 Maincy ☎ 01 64 14 41 90
🚈 Gare de Lyon to Melun then taxi

GOLF
Disneyland Paris
Close to the theme park and the Disneyland hotels (27 holes).
✉ Allée de la Mare Houleuse, 77700 Magny le Hongre ☎ 01 60 45 68 90
🚈 RER to Marne-la-Vallée/Chessy

HIKING
Comité Régional de Randonnée Pédestre en Île-de-France
Information on hiking in the Île de France.
✉ 40 rue de Paradis, 75010 Paris ☎ 01 48 01 81 51 🚈 Plaisance, Pernéty

HORSE-RACING
Hippodrome de Chantilly
Prix du Jockey-Club and Prix de Diane-Hermès in June.
✉ Route de l'Aigle, 60631 Chantilly ☎ 03 44 62 44 00 🚈 Gare du Nord to
Chantilly-Gouvieux

Index

Acknowledgements

The Automobile Association would like to thank the following photographers, companies and picture libraries for their assistance in the preparation of this book.

Abbreviations for the picture credits are as follows – (t) top; (b) bottom; (c) centre; (l) left; (r) right; (AA) AA World Travel Library.

4l Eiffel Tower, AA/B Reiger; **4c** Métro, AA/C Sawyer; **4r** Louvre, AA/J Tims; **5l** La Coupole, AA/B Reiger; **5c** Lafayette, AA/C Sawyer; **5r** Château de Fontainebleau, AA/M Jourdan; **6/7** Eiffel Tower, AA/B Reiger; **8/9** Musee d'Orsay, AA/M Jourdan; **10bl** Place de la Concorde, AA/K Paterson; **10br** Old poster, AA/T Souter; **10/1** Boulevard St-Michel, AA/C Sawyer; **11bl** Galerie Vivienne, AA/J Tims; **12bl** Croissant, AA/B Smith; **12br** Hediard and Fauchon, AA/T Souter; **13t** French bread, AA/C Sawyer; **13c** Jean-Paul Hevin chocolates, AA/C Sawyer; **13bl** Market, AA/M Jourdan; **13br** Camomile flowers, AA/B Smith; **14/5** Jean-Paul Hevin chocolates, AA/C Sawyer; **14** Market, AA/C Sawyer; **15bl** Wine, AA/B Reiger; **15br** Montmartre, AA/K Paterson; **16** Île St-Louis, AA/M Jourdan; **17** Les Deux Magots café, AA/M Jourdan; **18** Moulin-Rouge, AA/P Enticknap; **19** Sacré-Coeur, AA/T Souter; **20/1** Métro, AA/C Sawyer; **24** Jazz, Digitalvision; **26** Charles de Gaulle Airport, AA/C Sawyer; **26/7** Gare du Nord, AA/C Sawyer; **28** RER train station, AA/C Sawyer; **29** Bus, AA/M Jourdan; **30** Phonebox, AA/K Paterson; **34/5** Louvre, AA/ J Tims; **36** Centre Georges Pompidou, AA/W Voysey; **37t** Centre Georges Pompidou, AA/T Souter; **37b** Centre Georges Pompidou, AA/J Tims; **38t** Champs-Elysées, AA/P Kenward; **38c** Arc de Triomphe, AA/P Enticknap; **38b** Parc Monceau, AA/K Paterson; **38/9** Champs-Elysées, AA/M Jourdan; **40** La Grande Arche, AA/J Tims; **40/1** La Grande Arche, AA/T Souter; **41** La Grande Arche, AA/T Souter; **42** Les Invalides, AA/J Tims; **42/3** Les Invalides, AA/K Paterson; **43** Les Invalides AA/K Paterson; **44/5** Louvre, AA/M Jourdan; **46t** Candles, Notre-Dame, AA/T Souter; **46b** Notre-Dame, AA/C Sawyer; **46/7** Notre-Dame, AA/C Sawyer; **47** Notre-Dame, AA/T Souter; **48t** Musee d'Orsay, AA/M Jourdan; **48b** Musee d'Orsay, AA/M Jourdan; **48/9** Musee d'Orsay, AA/P Enticknap; **49** Musee d'Orsay, AA/M Jourdan; **50** River Seine, AA; **50/1** Île St-Louis, AA/C Sawyer; **52** Palais de Chaillot, AA/P Enticknap; **52/3** Eiffel Tower, AA/J Tims; **54/5** Parc de la Villette, AA/M Jourdan; **55t** Parc de la Villette, AA/M Jourdan; **55b** Parc de la Villette, AA/M Jourdan; **56/7** La Coupole, AA/B Reiger; **58/9** Café de Flore, AA/B Reiger; **60/1** Restaurant interior, AA/C Sawyer; **62** La Coupole, AA/C Sawyer; **64/5** Eiffel Tower, AA/M Jourdan; **66/7** Cité des Sciences, AA/J Tims; **68/9** Parc Astérix, Parc Astérix; **70/1** River Seine, AA/K Paterson; **72/3** Moulin-Rouge, AA/ **74/5** Musée Rodin, AA/M Jourdan; **76/7** Sacré-Coeur, AA/P Enticknap; **78/9** Hôtel Franklin Roosevelt, AA/C Sawyer; **80** Ladurée Shop, AA/C Sawyer; **80/1** Galeries Lafayette, AA/K Paterson; **82/3** Lafayette shopping bag, AA/C Sawyer; **85** Café life, AA/K Paterson; **86/7c** Salle de Gens, AA/K Paterson; **86/7b** Pont-Neuf, AA/T Souter; **88** Institut du Monde Arabe, AA/C Sawyer; **89** Institut du Monde Arabe, AA/M Jourdan; **90t** Musée National du Moyan-Age, AA/K Paterson; **90c** Musée de Cluny, AA/J Tims; **90/1** The Panthéon, AA/J Tims; **92** Jardin des Plantes, AA/T Souter; **93** Sainte-Chapelle, AA/J Tims; **94** River Seine, AA/M Jourdan; **100/1** Left Bank, AA/K Paterson; **102/3** Delacroix, museum, AA/J Tims; **105** Institut de France, AA/P Kenward; **106** Jardin du Luxembourg, AA/M Jourdan; **106/7** Montparnasse, AA; **108** Rodin Museum, AA/M Jourdan; **110** Église St-Sulpice, AA/M Jourdan; **118** Arc de Triomphe, AA/M Jourdan; **121** Place de la Concorde, AA/B Reiger; **122** Lavin shop window, AA/C Sawyer; **123** Grand Palais, AA/M Jourdan; **124** Musée Jacquemart-André, AA/P Kenward; **125** Musée Marmottan-Monet, AA/J Tims; **126** Musée Nissim de Camondo, AA/J Tims; **127** Palais Royal, AA/M Jourdan; **128** Jardin des Tuileries, AA/M Jourdan; **135** Place de Bastille, AA/K Paterson; **136/7** Opéra de Paris, AA/C Sawyer; **138/9** Musée Carnavalet, AA/K Paterson; **140/1c** Église St-Eustache, AA/J Tims; **140/1b** Les Halles, AA/M Jourdan; **142/3c** Le Marais, AA/C Sawyer; **142/3b** Hôtel de Ville, AA/M Jourdan; **144** Père Lachaise Cemetery, AA/M Jourdan; **145** Musée Picasso, AA/M Jourdan; **146t** Place des Vosges, AA/B Reiger; **146c** Place des Vosges, AA/K Paterson; **153** Montmartre, AA/M Jourdan; **154/5** Marché Aux Puces, AA/C Sawyer; **156/7** Cimetière de Montmartre, AA/P Kenward; **157** Moulin de la Galette, AA/M Jourdan; **158/9** Sacre Coeur, AA/J Tims; **160** Place de Tertre, AA/T Souter; **166/7** Château de Fontainebleau, AA/M Jourdan; **169** Château de Chantilly, AA/D Noble; **170** Château de Fontainebleau, AA/D Noble; **170/1** Parc Astérix, Parc Astérix; **172/3** Château de Vaux le Vicomte, AA/B Reiger; **174/5** Chateau de Versailles, AA/M Jourdan; **175t** Château de Versailles, AA/M Jourdan; **175b** Château de Versailles, AA/D Noble; **176** Forêt de Fontainebleau, AA/D Noble; **178** Château de Vincennes AA/J Tims.

Every effort has been made to trace the copyright holders, and we apologise in advance for any accidental errors. We would be happy to apply the corrections in the following edition of this publication.

Street Index

Dear Reader

Your comments, opinions and recommendations are very important to us. So please help us to improve our travel guides by taking a few minutes to complete this simple questionnaire.

You do not need a stamp (unless posted outside the UK). If you do not want to cut this page from your guide, then photocopy it or write your answers on a plain sheet of paper.

Send to: **The Editor, AA World Travel Guides,**
FREEPOST SCE 4598, Basingstoke RG21 4GY.

Your recommendations...

We always encourage readers' recommendations for restaurants, nightlife or shopping – if your recommendation is used in the next edition of the guide, we will send you a **FREE AA Guide** of your choice from this series. Please state below the establishment name, location and your reasons for recommending it.

_____
_____
_____
_____
_____
_____

Please send me **AA Guide** _____

About this guide...

Which title did you buy?

   AA _____

Where did you buy it?_____

When? <u>m m</u> / <u>y y</u>

Why did you choose this guide? _____

_____
_____
_____
_____

Did this guide meet your expectations?

Exceeded ☐   Met all ☐   Met most ☐   Fell below ☐

Were there any aspects of this guide that you particularly liked? _____

_____
_____
_____

continued on next page...

Is there anything we could have done better? _____
_____
_____
_____

About you...
Name (*Mr/Mrs/Ms*) _____
Address _____
_____
_____ Postcode

Daytime tel nos _____
Email _____

Please only give us your mobile phone number or email if you wish to hear from us about
other products and services from the AA and partners by text or mms, or email.

Which age group are you in?
Under 25 ☐   25–34 ☐   35–44 ☐   45–54 ☐   55–64 ☐   65+ ☐

How many trips do you make a year?
Less than one ☐   One ☐   Two ☐   Three or more ☐

Are you an AA member? Yes ☐   No ☐

About your trip...
When did you book? m m / y y   When did you travel? m m / y y

How long did you stay? _____

Was it for business or leisure? _____

Did you buy any other travel guides for your trip?

If yes, which ones? _____
_____
_____

Thank you for taking the time to complete this questionnaire. Please send it to us as soon as
possible, and remember, you do not need a stamp (*unless posted outside the UK*).

AA Travel Insurance call 0800 072 4168 or visit www.theAA.com